KU-251-956

The Story of a Life

The Story of a Life

AHARON APPELFELD

Translated from the Hebrew
by Aloma Halter

HAMISH HAMILTON
an imprint of
PENGUIN BOOKS

HAMISH HAMILTON

Published by the Penguin Group
Penguin Books Ltd, 80 Strand, London WC2R ORL, England
Penguin Group (USA) Inc., 375 Hudson Street, New York, New York 10014, USA
Penguin Group (Canada), 90 Eglinton Avenue East, Suite 700, Toronto, Ontario, Canada M4P 3YZ
(a division of Pearson Penguin Canada Inc.)
Penguin Ireland, 25 St Stephen's Green, Dublin 2, Ireland (a division of Penguin Books Ltd)
Penguin Group (Australia), 250 Camberwell Road, Camberwell, Victoria 3124, Australia
(a division of Pearson Australia Group Pty Ltd)
Penguin Books India Pvt Ltd, 11 Community Centre, Panchsheel Park, New Delhi – 110 017, India
Penguin Group (NZ), cnr Airborne and Rosedale Roads, Albany,
Auckland 1310, New Zealand (a division of Pearson New Zealand Ltd)
Penguin Books (South Africa) (Pty) Ltd, 24 Sturdee Avenue, Rosebank 2196, Johannesburg, South Africa

Penguin Books Ltd, Registered Offices: 80 Strand, London WC2R ORL, England

www.penguin.com

First published by Shocken Books 2004
Published by Hamish Hamilton 2005
1

Copyright © Aharon Appelfeld, 2004
Translation copyright © Shocken Books, 2004

The moral right of the author has been asserted

Printed in Great Britain by Clays Ltd, St Ives plc

A CIP catalogue record for this book is available from the British Library

ISBN 0-241-14319-5

Preface

THE PAGES BEFORE YOU are segments of contemplation and memory. Memory is elusive and selective; it holds on to what it chooses to hold on to. I won't say that it retains only what is good and pleasant. Very like a dream, memory takes specific details out of the viscous flow of events—sometimes tiny, seemingly insignificant details—stores them deeply away, and at certain times brings them up to the surface. Like a dream, memory also tries to imbue events with some meaning.

Ever since my childhood, I have felt that memory is a living and effervescent reservoir that animates my being. When I was still a child, I would sit and visualize the summer holidays at my grandparents' home in the country. For hours I'd sit by the window and picture the journey there. Everything that I recalled from previous vacations would return to me in the most vivid way.

Memory and imagination sometimes dwell together. In those long-buried years it was as if they competed. Memory was tangible, as if solid. Imagination had wings. Memory pulled toward the known, and imagination sailed toward the unknown. Memory always brought me pleasure and tranquillity. Imagination would take me from place to place, but eventually would depress me.

At times I learned that there are people who live solely by the power of imagination. My uncle Herbert was like that. He had inherited considerable wealth, but because he lived in a world of imagination, he wasted everything and was completely impoverished. When I got to know him better, he was already a poor man, living off the goodwill of his family, but even in his poverty he did not cease to dream. His gaze would be fixed far beyond you, and he always spoke about the future, as if the present or the past didn't exist.

It's amazing how clear even my most distant and hidden childhood memories can be, in particular those connected to the Carpathian Mountains and the broad plains stretching out at their foothills. During those last vacations before the war, our eyes would devour the mountains and plains with a fearsome longing, as if my parents knew that these were the last holidays, and that from now on life would be hell.

When World War II broke out, I was seven years old. The sequence of time became confused—no more summer and winter, no more long visits to my grandparents in the country. Our life was now crammed into a narrow room. For some time we were in the ghetto, and at the end of autumn we were thrown out of it. For weeks we were on the road, and then, eventually, in the camp, from which I managed to escape.

During the war I was not myself, but like a small creature that has a burrow, or, more precisely, a few burrows. Thoughts and feelings were greatly constricted. In truth, sometimes there welled up within me a painful sense of astonishment at why I had been left alone. But these reflections would fade with the mists of the forest, and the animal within me would return and wrap me in its fur. Of the war years I remember little, as if they were not six consecutive years. It's true that sometimes images surface from the heavy mist: a dark figure, a hand that had been charred, a shoe of which nothing was left but shreds. These pictures, sometimes as fierce as the blast from a furnace, fade away quickly, as if refusing to reveal themselves, and again there's the same black tunnel that we call the war. This is the limit of conscious memory. But the palms of one's hands, the soles of one's feet, one's back, and one's knees remember more than memory. Had I known how to draw from them, I would have been overwhelmed with what I have seen. On some occasions I have been able to listen to my body, and then I would write a few chapters, but even they are just fragments of a pulsing darkness that will always be locked inside me.

After the war, I was on the Italian coast for some months and then spent some time on the Yugoslavian coast. Those were months of wonderful oblivion. The water, the sun, and the sand kneaded and soothed us until nightfall. And at night we would sit by the fire, frying fish and drinking coffee. Roaming around the beaches were all kinds of people who had been affected by the war: musicians, jugglers, opera singers, actors, gloomy fortune-tellers, smugglers, and thieves. Among this motley crowd there were also child artists, only six or seven years old, who were adopted by corrupt "managers" who would drag them around from place to place. Every night there would be a performance, sometimes even two.

Then oblivion constructed its deeply fortified basements, and soon after that, we took them to Palestine. When we arrived there, oblivion was already solidified in all of us.

From this standpoint, Israel was a kind of continuation of Italy. Oblivion found fertile ground. Of course, the ideology prevalent in those years aided and abetted this locking up of memory, but the command to erect walls did not come from the outside only. Sometimes things I'd seen during the war would slip through from the walled-in basements of memory, demanding the right to exist. But they did not have the power to bring down the pillars of oblivion and the will to live. And life itself said then: Forget! Be absorbed! The kibbutzim and the various youth villages were veritable greenhouses for cultivating oblivion.

For many years I was sunk deep within the slumber of oblivion. My life flowed on the surface. I grew used to the cramped and moldy basements within me. True, I was always afraid of them. It seemed to me, not without reason, that the dark creatures seething there were growing stronger, and that someday, when the place became too narrow for them, they would burst out onto the surface. And, indeed, such outbursts did occur from time to time, but the powers of suppression held them in, and the basement was again shut up under lock and key.

For how many years did this continue—this distance, this division from *there* to *here*, from below to above? The story of this struggle is in these pages, and it stretches across a broad canvas: memory and oblivion, the sense of chaos and impotence on one side and the desire for a meaningful life on the other. This is not a book that asks questions and responds to them. These pages are a description of a struggle, if one can borrow Kafka's expression. All aspects of the soul join in this struggle: the memory of home and of parents, the sheer pastoral beauty of the Carpathians, my grandparents, and the many lights that streamed into my soul. After them came the war and all the destruction it wrought, and the scars that it left. And, finally, the long years in Israel: working the land, learning the language, overcoming the confusion of youth, attending university, and beginning to write.

This book is not a summary, but an attempt (and perhaps a desperate attempt) to integrate the different parts of my life and to reconnect them to the wellsprings of their being. The reader should not expect a sequential and precise account in this story of a life. These are the regions of my life that have been packed together in memory, and they are alive and pulsating. Much has been lost and much corroded by oblivion. At first it seemed that very little remained, and yet, when I laid one piece alongside another, I saw that not only have they been made whole by the years, but they have even achieved some level of meaning.

The Story of a Life

1

AT WHAT POINT does my memory begin? It sometimes seems to me as if it began only when I was four, when we set off for the first time, Mother, Father, and I, for a vacation into the heart of the shadowy, moist forests of the Carpathians. But I sometimes think that memory began to bud from within me before that, in my room, next to the double-glazed window that was decorated with paper flowers. Snow is falling, and fleecy soft flakes are slowly coming down from the sky with a sound so faint that you cannot hear it. For hours I sit and gaze in wonder, until I merge with the white flow and drift off to sleep.

A clearer memory is linked for me to one word, too long and rather hard to pronounce, *Erdbeeren*, which means "strawberries" in German. It is spring. Mother is standing at the open window. I am perched on a chair next to her, and suddenly, from a side alley, there appears a young Ruthenian girl. She is carrying a broad, circular wicker basket full of strawberries on her head. *"Erdbeeren!"* Mother calls out. Her call is not directed at the girl but at Father, who is in the back garden and very near the girl. Father stops her, she lifts the basket off her head, and they speak for a moment. Father laughs, draws out a banknote from the pocket of his jacket, and presents it to the girl, who, in exchange, gives him the basket with all the strawberries inside it. Father comes up the steps and enters·the house. Now one can see it close up: the basket is not deep but extremely wide; the berries are tiny and red and still alive with the scent of the forest. I so want to put out my hand and take a handful from the basket, but I know that this is completely forbidden, and I restrain myself. Still, my mother understands me, and she takes a handful from the basket, rinses them, and serves me them in a small bowl. I'm so happy that I can hardly breathe.

Here the ritual begins: Mother sprinkles powdered sugar on the tiny fruit, adds cream, and serves up the delicacy to each of us. There's no need to ask for another portion: Mother ladles it out, more and more, and we feast on it with great relish, as if we are about to finish the strawberries. But there is nothing to worry about, the basket is still full, and even if we go on eating all through the night, it won't get any emptier. "A pity there are no guests," says Mother. Father laughs quietly, as if a partner to a conspiracy. And the following day, too, we eat more overflowing portions, though distractedly and no longer with a ravenous appetite. Mother puts the remaining strawberries in the pantry. Later I saw, with my very own eyes, how the glorious berries had turned grayish and had shriveled up; for the rest of the day, I felt sad whenever I remembered them. But the woven basket, made of simple twigs, remained in our home for many days, and every time I glanced at it, I would remember how it had looked like a red crown when it rested on the head of the Ruthenian peasant girl.

. . .

CLEARER MEMORIES are the walks along the banks of the river, on the paths by the fields, and on the grassy meadows. I see us climb a hill, sit on top of it, and gaze around. Speaking little, my parents listen attentively. With Mother it is more obvious. When she listens, her large eyes are wide open, as if trying to take in everything around her. At home, too, there is more quiet than talking. Nothing spoken—no phrases—remain in my memory from those distant days, only Mother's gaze. It was filled with so much softness and tender solicitude that I feel it to this very day.

OUR HOUSE IS SPACIOUS and has many rooms. One balcony faces the street, and the other one, the public park. The drapes are long, trailing on the parquet floor. When the maid changes them, a scent of starch fills the whole house. But even more than the drapes, I love the floor—or, rather, the carpet that covers the floor. On its floral patterns I construct streets and houses from wooden blocks and populate them with stuffed bears and tin dogs. The carpet is thick and soft, and I sink into it for hours, pretending that I'm traveling on a train, crossing continents, and eventually arriving at my grandfather's village.

In summer we will travel to Grandfather's village, and just thinking of it induces a sort of drowsiness, as memories of the previous visit surface. But the images I see in my memory have become so hazy since then that they are more like a dream. All the same, one word remains, and that is *mestameh*—"presumably." The word is strange and incomprehensible, yet Grandmother repeats it several times a day. Many times I was about to ask what this strange word meant, but I didn't. Mother and I speak German. Sometimes it seems to me that the way Grandfather and Grandmother talk makes Mother uncomfortable, and that she'd prefer for me not to hear their language. All the same, I summon up the courage and ask, "What's the language that Grandfather and Grandmother are speaking?"

"Yiddish," Mother whispers in my ear.

DAYS IN THE VILLAGE are long, stretching deep into the white night. In the village there are no carpets, only mats. Even the guest room has a mat. At the touch of a foot, the mat makes a dry rustling sound. Mother sits next to me and carves into a watermelon. In the village there are no restaurants and no cinema; we sit out in the yard till late, watching the sunset that goes on till the middle of the night. I try hard not to doze off, but eventually I fall asleep.

Here the days are full of small enchantments. A band of three Gypsies suddenly enters the yard and bursts into the sad strains of violin music. Grandmother doesn't lose her temper; she knows them well and lets them go on. Their playing makes me sadder and sadder, and I want to cry. Mother helps out and asks the Gypsies to stop playing, but they won't. "Don't stop us! This is the way we Gypsies pray!"

"But it's frightening for the child," Mother implores.

"There's nothing to fear—we're not devils."

Eventually Mother gives them a banknote, and they stop playing. One of the Gypsies tries to come up and be nice to me, but Mother keeps him at a distance.

Just as the Gypsies have left the back yard, a chimney sweep appears. A tall man, with black cables wound completely around his torso, he sets to work without delay. His face is all sooty, and when he stands by the chimney flue he looks like one of those demons from the tales of the Brothers Grimm that Mother reads me before I go to sleep. I want to let Mother in on this secret, but I hesitate.

Toward evening, the cows come back from the pasture. The lowing and mooing and the dust fill the air with melancholy, but this is soon dispelled by the nightly ritual of boiling up preserves. Plum jam, pear-and-plum jam, ripe-cherry jam—each jam has its appointed hour of the night. Grandmother takes a large copper pot from the kitchen and puts it on the garden bonfire, which has been kindled since twilight. Now the copper pot is gleaming golden. The boiling goes on for most of the night. Grandmother tastes and stirs, adds laurel leaves, and eventually serves me a dish of warm jam. The sweetness, for which I have waited so eagerly, brings me no happiness this time. The fear that the night will end and that in the morning we will have to climb into a carriage to return to the city—this fear now grips me, stealthily spoiling my happiness. I take Mother's hand and kiss it, kiss it again and again, until, intoxicated with all the night scents, I fall asleep on the rush mat.

In the country, I'm with Mother. Father remains in the city to run the business, and when he suddenly appears, he seems alien to me. With Mother I go out to the meadows by the river, or, rather, by one of the streams of the River Prut. The waters flow slowly, the clearness is dazzling, and one's feet sink into the soft ground.

In the summer, days stretch out slowly and without end. I know how to count up to forty, to draw flowers, and in another day or two I'll know how to write my name in block letters. Mother doesn't leave me for a moment. Her closeness is so wonderful that even a moment without her makes me sad.

Sometimes, unexpectedly, I ask her about God, or about

when I was born. Mother is embarrassed by these questions, and it seems to me that she blushes. On one occasion she tells me, "God is in the sky, and He knows everything." The answer delights me as much as if I had been presented with an enchanted gift. But for the most part her answers are short, as if she simply has to discharge a duty. Sometimes I keep on asking, but it doesn't make her talk more.

UNLIKE MOTHER, Grandmother is a large and sturdy woman, and when she places her two hands on the broad wooden table, they fill it. As she talks, she describes things, and you can tell that she loves what she's describing: the vegetables in the garden, for example, or the orchard behind the cowshed. It's hard to understand how Grandmother can be my mother's mother. Next to her, Mother looks like a pale shadow. Grandmother frequently scolds her daughter for leaving some of her soup in the bowl, or a piece of vegetable pie on her plate. Grandmother has firm views on everything: how to grow vegetables, when to pick plums, who is an honest man and who is not. When it comes to children, her convictions are even firmer: children should go to bed before dark, and not at 9 p.m. Mother, on the other hand, doesn't see any harm in a child falling asleep on the straw matting.

Grandmother isn't always in a decisive mood. Sometimes she closes her eyes tight, seems to sink into her large body, and tells Mother about bygone days. I understand nothing of what she says, and yet I enjoy listening to her. When she picks me up and lifts me high above her head, I feel as weak as if I were still a baby.

Grandfather is tall and thin and seldom speaks. He leaves for prayers early in the morning, and when he returns, the table is laden with vegetables, cheeses, and fried eggs.

Grandfather's presence imparts silence to us all. He does not
look at us and we do not look at him, but on the Sabbath eve
his face softens. Grandmother irons a white shirt for him, and
we set out for the synagogue.

The walk to the synagogue is long and full of wonders.
A horse stands in astonishment, and there is a small girl next
to it, about my height. She also stands and stares. Not far from
them, a foal is rolling on the grass. The strong, barrel-like
creature is stretched on its back, waving its legs in the air as if
it has been toppled and is thrashing about, as I sometimes do.
Then, just to show everyone that it wasn't knocked down, it
gets back up. There is astonishment in the dozens of pairs of
eyes of the horses, sheep, and goats who are all following the
foal's movements, happy that it's back on its feet.

Grandfather walks in silence, but his silence is not
frightening. We move along fast but stop every few minutes.
And for a moment it seems to me that he wants to show me
something and to name it, the way Father does. I am wrong.
Grandfather continues in silence, and what escapes from his
mouth is swallowed up and not comprehensible, but then he
lets some words escape that I can understand. "God," he says,
"is in the sky and there is nothing to fear." The gestures that
go with the words are even clearer than the words themselves.

Grandfather's synagogue is small and made of wood. By
the light of day it resembles a roadside chapel, but it's longer
and has no statues or objects on the shelves. The entrance is
low, and Grandfather has to stoop to enter. I follow. Here a
surprise awaits us: many golden candles are stuck into two
troughs of sand and radiate a diffused light along with the
scent of beeswax.

The prayers are almost silent. Grandfather prays with
his eyes closed, and the candlelight flickers on his forehead.
All those praying are absorbed in their prayer. Not me. For

some reason I have suddenly remembered the city, the damp
streets after the rain. In the summer, sudden showers fall, and
Father drags me after him, down narrow alleys, from one
square to another. Father doesn't go to synagogue; he is pas-
sionate about natural beauty, and he also loves unusual buildings, churches, chapels, and cafés where they serve coffee in
fine cups.

Grandfather breaks into my imaginings. He bends
down and shows me the prayer book, the yellow pages with
the large black letters leaping out from within it.

All the movements here are careful and secretive. I
don't understand anything. For a moment it seems to me that
the lions that are above the Holy Ark are about to stir and
leap down. The prayers are conducted in whispers. Sometimes
a louder voice rises on the swell, dragging the whisperers after
it. This is the home of God, and people come here in order to
sense His presence. Only I don't know how to talk to Him. If I
knew how to read the prayer book, I would also be able to see
the wonders and the secrets, but for right now I have to hide
myself away so that God won't see my ignorance.

The man leading the prayers reads and embellishes and
reads—and as he does, he skips over some passages, bowing to
the right and to the left. He's nearest to the Holy Ark and
tries to influence God; all the others also raise their heads,
subjugating their will to the will of God.

While this is going on, the candles stuck in the sand
troughs burn out, and then the men take off their prayer
shawls and a kind of quiet wonderment shines in their eyes, as
if they understand something they didn't understand before.

Leaving the synagogue takes a long time. The elderly
leave first, and only then do all the others file out. I already
want to be outside, where the air is clear and people talk to
one another, not to God.

Once again, we're on our way. Grandfather hums a prayer, but it's a different kind of prayer, not strained, and with a more casual melody. The sky is full of stars; their light spills onto our heads. Grandfather says that one should hurry toward the synagogue but walk slowly away from it. I don't understand why, but I don't ask. I've already noticed: Grandfather doesn't like questions and explanations. Whenever I ask a question, silence descends, answers are slow in coming, and even when they do, they're extremely brief. That no longer bothers me now. I have also learned to remain silent and listen to the subtle sounds that surround me. The sounds here, unlike those in the city, are frequent but low, even if sometimes the darkness is torn by the screeching of a bird.

We walk on for about an hour, and when we approach the house, Grandmother meets us; she's also dressed in white. Mother and I are wearing our usual clothes. The Kiddush and the festive meal are quiet, like a prayer; only the four of us are about to receive God and the Sabbath.

Mother, for some reason, is always melancholy at the Sabbath table. Sometimes it seems to me that she once knew how to talk to God in her language, like Grandfather and Grandmother, but because of some misunderstanding, she has forgotten that language. On the Sabbath eve, this sorrow weighs on her.

After the Sabbath meal, we take a stroll to the stream. Grandfather and Grandmother walk ahead, and we follow behind them. At night this branch of the river looks wider. The darkness sinks, and white skies open above us, flowing slowly. I stretch out my hands and feel the white flow coming straight into my palms.

"Mother," I say.

"What is it, my love?"

The words that I had sought to describe the sensation

have slipped away from me. Since I don't have words, I sit there, open my eyes wide, and let the white night flow into me.

THE PRAYERS ON THE SABBATH EVE are only a preparation for the prayers on the Sabbath day, which go on for many hours. Grandfather is completely immersed in the prayer book, and I sit next to him and see God come and sit between the lions that are on the Holy Ark. I'm astonished that Grandfather does not seem to get excited about something so awesome and wonderful.

"Grandfather—" I can no longer contain myself. Grandfather puts his finger to his lips and doesn't allow me to ask.

After some time, two men go up to the Ark, and God, who had been sitting between the lions, is gone. His disappearance is so hasty that it's as if He wasn't ever there. The two short men are not content with that: they open the Ark. Now the Ark is wide open and prayers flow straight into it. At this point in the proceedings, I feel very sorry that I don't know how to pray. Two children of around my age are already standing and praying like grown-ups. They already know how to speak to God, and only I am mute. Sadness at this lack of speech wells up within me, increasing from moment to moment, and I remember the park in the city where I sometimes sit with Father. It is a park where there are no wonders. People sit quietly on the benches. They are quiet because they don't know how to pray, I realize, and I snap to attention. It is at just this moment that the Torah scroll is being taken out of the Ark and lifted high. All eyes are turned to the Torah, and a shiver goes down my back.

The reading from the Torah on the *bima*, the platform

in the middle of the synagogue, is like a secret within a secret. Now it seems to me that when all this whispering of secrets comes to an end, all these people will disappear and I'll be left alone, face-to-face with God, who lives in the Holy Ark. Four people surround the Torah, speaking to it as if God were tangible in this parchment scroll. For a moment I'm astonished that God—who's so immense—has squeezed Himself into this tiny platform.

After this, they roll up the Torah and sing with tremendous enthusiasm. The four people who stood on the *bima* raise their voices, as if trying to obliterate themselves. When the singing is finished, the Torah is raised and then returned to the Holy Ark. The Ark is closed, and the *parochet*, the embroidered curtain, seems to lock it in. For a moment I think that this has been a dream, and that when I awake from it Father will carry me away from this magic, and we'll return to the city, back to the broad intersecting streets and our house, which I love so much.

"Why don't you go outside?" Grandfather's whisper releases me.

I stand outside next to two tall trees and feel that I had been far from myself, from my own dreams, that I visited an unknown imagination, and that it's good that I left and returned to myself, next to the trees that cast their heavy shadows on the ground.

Again I look at the way the synagogue is built. The structure is so shaky that, were it not for the ivy that envelops it and holds it together, it's doubtful whether it could stand on its own rickety limbs. Suddenly I'm gripped by a great, unknown fear—a fear that in a moment the people will come out of the building, catch hold of me, and drag me inside. This fear is so tangible that I can feel the fingers of strangers pressing and poking me, and even the deep scratches.

"Father!" The cry escapes from my mouth, and I start to run. After I have run part of the way, the fear leaves me and I return to the two trees at the entrance to the synagogue. Now the prayers are quiet, and I go inside. Grandfather is deep in prayer and does not notice that I've come in. I stand next to him and look at the Holy Ark, which still seems locked up by the heavy embroidered curtain. I try to take in one word from the many words with which the men are talking to God, but I cannot. It's clear now: I cannot speak. Everyone is whispering, trying hard, and only I am without words. I stare, even though my eyes smart. I will never be able to ask anything of God, because I don't know how to talk in His language. My father and mother don't know how to talk in His language, either. Father has already told me once, "We have nothing but what our eyes can see." At the time I didn't understand this, but now it seems to me that I have guessed what it means.

The prayers have come to an end, though I don't realize it. The last prayer is said amid great enthusiasm, as if it is all about to begin anew. That is the ending, and those praying get to their feet. One of the old men comes up to me and asks me what my name is. I am scared, and I hold on tight to Grandfather's coat. The old man gazes at me and doesn't ask me anything else. Then little honey cakes and small glasses of cognac are served, and blessings, mingling with the smell of alcohol, waft up into the air.

After this we set out on the verdant path homeward. The sun is shining, and herds graze on the pastures. The sight reminds me of a different quiet in another place, but I do not know where. We cross the meadows and enter a sparse forest. There are a few abandoned buildings in the forest. Darkness crouches in their gaping entrances. Along the way we meet a Ruthenian peasant, an acquaintance of Grandfather's. They talk, and I don't understand a word. After that we stand on

the ridge of a hill, and there seems to be great agitation—
a movement across the cornfields.

As we approach the house, I see Mother, dressed in
white, standing at the entrance. It seems to me that she is
about to take off, to fly straight toward me. This time I am
right. With one swift movement, as if it weren't Mother but
a young Ruthenian girl, she runs toward us. Only seconds
later, I am in her arms. For a moment we are together in the
high grass.

In the afternoon we sit in the yard, and Grandmother
brings us long rolls and strawberries in cream. Mother is beautiful, with her hair loose over her shoulders and lights
sparkling on her long poplin dress, and I say in my innermost
being: That's how it will be from now on. Yet, even as I am
immersed in this hidden joy, sorrow constricts my heart, so
slight that I almost don't feel it, though, slowly and imperceptibly, it spreads inside me. I burst out crying, and Mother, who
is in a wonderful mood, gathers me in her arms. But I am
gripped, locked in this sadness and fear, and I refuse to be con-
soled. The fit of crying seizes me, and I know that this is the
last summer in the village, that henceforth the light will be
dimmed and darkness will seal the windows.

And so it is that, at night, after the Sabbath, Father
arrives, bringing with him the hustle and bustle of the big
city. Mother hastily packs the suitcases, and Grandmother
brings out a full crate of preserves covered in white gauze, a
crate of red apples, and two bottles of cherry liqueur that she
has made herself. The carriage is a fine one, but it doesn't
have extra room for all this produce, and the driver can barely
cram the precious gifts into the dark space under the seats.
Grandfather stands by the door, as if uprooted from the world
that he has been in. A gloomy sort of dismay radiates from his
eyes. He embraces Mother with great tenderness.

We set out in the carriage at a gallop in order to catch the last train. On the train I am again seized by a fit of crying, and Mother tries with all her might to calm me down, but the tears gush out of me and wet my shirt. Father's patience snaps, and he demands to know the reason for my tears. Though my sorrow is piercing and the pain seems immense, I don't have a single word to explain it. Father's anger increases. Eventually he can't contain himself and says, "If you don't stop crying, I'll slap you. You're five years old, and a child of five shouldn't cry without a reason."

This time Father, who almost never got angry and always remembered to bring me presents whenever he returned from a trip, is so frightening that my tears ceased. But Mother, who understands my pain, embraces me and draws me close to her. I drop into her lap and fall asleep.

2

MY MOTHER'S UNCLE, Uncle Felix, was a tall man, strong and quiet. He was the owner of an estate that extended over broad fields, grazing pastures, and forests. He even had a lake of his own. His house lay at the heart of the estate, surrounded by guest houses, offices, and servants' quarters.

Mother and I would visit him in spring and in summer, spending a week or two with him. Outwardly his appearance was completely secular, but his library was full of religious texts, of which several were first editions. Before he would open a Hebrew book, he would place a *kippah* on his head. There were two religious precepts to which he adhered strictly all the days of his life: praying and learning a page of Talmud daily. When he was wrapped in a prayer shawl and phylacteries, his freethinking appearance would fall away in an instant. Immersed in prayer, he looked just like an observant Jew. His manner of studying was also that of an observant Jew, learning to the singsong melody. His level of privacy was such that only few knew about this, and on the outside there

were no visible signs of a believer. He dressed like most landlords who were owners of large estates, in a suit, a white shirt,
and a tie that matched the suit. But, unlike most landlords,
he had refined taste. His suit had a quiet elegance that was
immediately discernible.

He spoke many languages and was careful to pronounce
them correctly. The German he spoke was flawless, and the
articles that he wrote on agricultural matters had been published not only in Czernowitz, the capital, but also in Lemberg and in Kraków, and they had been praised for their
precise language and clear style. By profession, Uncle Felix
was an agronomist, but the scope of his education was far
broader. He had a bookcase just for works of philosophy, a
bookcase of linguistic tomes, and a few bookcases of literature, not to mention the collection of his agricultural books,
which I loved leafing through. I would find within them pictures of fields, orchards, animals, and forests. Uncle Felix
always allowed me to look through the books in his library,
because he knew that I didn't tear books and that I turned the
pages very carefully.

Sometimes it seemed to me that horses were his greatest
love. On the estate there was a stable full of proud, tall, riding
horses tended by two stable hands. Even though he was no
longer young, Uncle Felix could mount a horse without help
from anyone. On a few occasions his grooms hoisted me up
and I rode with him. I was afraid, but the fear was mixed with
so much pleasure that it quickly receded. We'd ride across
fields and meadows until we reached the forest. Deep inside
the forest was a lake. Although it was extremely wide, toward
evening it would appear to be inward-looking and fathomless,
and the dusk flickering on its dark surface made it look like
the huge eye of some fearsome animal. On our return, Mother
would be waiting to welcome us with a joyful greeting. I was
four, or perhaps four and a half years old.

I didn't see much of my uncle's wife, Aunt Regina. A sickly woman, she spent most of the day resting in her room. The maid who took care of her so resembled her that they could have been sisters. The difference was that Aunt Regina lay in her bed, while the maid took care of her with great devotion, day and night. Aunt Regina's spacious room was steeped in an atmosphere of majesty and fear, perhaps because of the gloom that filled it, even during warm summer days. I hardly spoke with her. She would look at me but never ask me anything. Apparently, her mind had been dulled by pain, or perhaps in her delirium she didn't see me. Aunt Regina knew a lot about French literature, and in her youth had written a small book on Stendhal. My mother didn't like her, but had a high regard for her education.

Uncle Felix's pride and joy were the pictures that he'd acquired in Vienna and in Paris—among them, a Modigliani, a Matisse print, and some superb watercolors. The pictures matched the delicate furniture of the house perfectly. Wealthy Jews of Uncle Felix's generation choked their rooms with expensive and cumbersome furniture; they hung sentimental oil paintings on the walls; their drawing rooms overflowed with vases and stuffed animals; and on their floors they laid heavy, rather vulgar carpets. Uncle Felix knew these wealthy Jews all too well—their greed and their materialism—and when he was in the mood, he'd imitate them. He particularly loved to mimic the broken German they spoke, their ignorance in matters of Jewish learning, their vulgar style of dressing, and their behavior, so lacking in all politeness. He even mocked the way they treated their wives. He was repulsed by them and would keep his distance.

Uncle Felix had no children. In their youth, the couple had adopted a Ruthenian child and looked after him with great devotion. At the age of seven the child escaped, running back to his village and to his insane mother. He refused to return to his adoptive parents. I kept asking my mother about the Ruthenian boy. Mother told me a little, but without details. For some reason I identified with the child and pictured him fleeing from Uncle's house to his mother's hut.

SOMETIMES WE'D COME to visit in winter as well. In the winter there were clouds covering the estate, and snow fell incessantly. I loved to sit by the blazing stove, listening to the crackle of firewood. In the summer the days were long and stretched deep into the nights, but in winter the days were as short as a passing breeze. The brief light was grayish and faded in the middle of day.

Evenings on Uncle Felix's estate were full of small meals. At four o'clock there was tea, with pear cake decorated with cherries, and at seven o'clock, a splendid supper. We would linger over the meals, and we would be filled with the surrounding silence. In Uncle Felix's home people spoke little and seldom argued; useless theories were never aired. Most evenings were spent reading or listening to music. I have been in many quiet homes, but the quiet inside Uncle Felix's home had a special quality; it was a quiet that welled up from within the place itself and surrounded one with a pleasant awareness.

Sometimes Aunt Regina would get up from her sickbed and appear in the drawing room. Uncle Felix would rise to greet her. Apparently, her pains were almost unbearable. Occasionally there was nothing to do except call the doctor, but generally the maid who cared for her would persuade her to return to her bed and would rub her back and her legs, assuring her that she'd soon feel better.

Aunt Regina wasn't used to strange people. Once she appeared in the drawing room and saw me sitting on the floor, leafing through a book. "Who's the child?" she said, turning to her maid, as if I weren't her nephew but some strange child. Still, apart from such unpleasant incidents, the days on my uncle's estate passed quietly and without disturbance.

Uncle Felix was a pleasant and generous manager. No worker ever complained that he had not been given the wages he deserved. My uncle's policies reflected his liberal philosophy: give more to the workers and you'll get more in return. He was very wealthy, but not a miser like the *nouveaux riches*, whose stinginess blinded them to the needs of others.

There were also fine days in winter, days drenched in sunshine, and we would set out on sleds to speed down the hillsides. Sometimes my father would also join us in these adventures. I would be installed at a vantage point from which I could see the sledding. Uncle Felix excelled at this, too. Despite his age, he would sled around the bend like a young man. Father and Mother might topple off, but not Uncle Felix.

Even the trees on Uncle Felix's estate were taller than the ones I was used to seeing; the landscape was more lush and the servants seemed taller, almost touching the ceiling. Uncle Felix's life and his estate were legendary; most of the stories were pleasant, but some were frightening. There was a drunkard who had gone berserk, ax in hand, cursing the Jews and their wealth and scaring away the maidservants with his threats; and there was a horse who'd thrown off the stable boy, bolted from the stable, and went crazy in the yard. On one of my summer visits, a baby was laid on the doorstep of the house during the night; the servants discovered the bundle in the morning and called my uncle.

On his estate the quiet was deep but not absolute. The night air would be torn by the calls of birds of prey, and wolves howled. Uncle Felix had a forthright attitude toward nature. From childhood he'd loved plants and animals. His father, an elderly rabbi, did not look kindly upon his lifestyle or his occupation, but neither did he preach to him, because he also had a kind of hidden yearning for animals: he kept bees in his garden.

In the summer of 1937, life changed beyond recognition. The government became anti-Semitic, and the police sided with the rabble and the underworld. Boundaries were swept away, and robbery became a nightly occurrence. Uncle Felix—who had lived on the estate since his youth, had built the house, cultivated the fields, and preserved the forests, and had mingled in non-Jewish society—tried not only to hold on but also to fight back. At night he'd put on his wool cap and go out to chase away the thieves. One night he caught a youth of around fifteen who swore on the life of Jesus that he would never steal again. Uncle Felix was not satisfied with this oath and insisted upon a specific pledge. Out of sheer terror, the youth fell on his knees, pleaded, and then burst into bleating sobs. Uncle Felix let him go, and, like an animal suddenly released, the youth bolted in the direction of the gate.

Aunt Regina passed away that summer, and in accordance with her wishes, there was a secular funeral. She had asked to be buried on the estate, on one of the hillocks that overlooked the valley and its little brooks. Uncle Felix, who had loved her and her whims, took great care to carry out her wishes exactly as she had requested. Poems by Rilke were read aloud at her grave, armfuls of flowers were placed there, and a quartet played Mozart sonatas. The quartet, which had been brought over from Czernowitz, played morning and night throughout the entire seven days of mourning. Aunt Regina had left a list of compositions, and it was in this order that they were played.

Aunt Regina hated Orthodox Jewish rituals. For years Uncle Felix had tried to change her mind. Once a Jew arrived at the estate in traditional garb. When she saw him, she began shouting hysterically, as if the house had been infiltrated by ghosts.

After Aunt Regina's death, Uncle Felix changed, becoming increasingly withdrawn. Sometimes he'd come into town and sit in our drawing room and drink lemon tea. Father and Mother adored him. We knew he was knowledgeable in many fields, but his knowledge wasn't flaunted, and he was never opinionated or full of himself. He would bring me special toys and talk to me as if I were already grown up, because he had a theory that children are endowed with a keen sensibility and natural intelligence and that they should be listened to. He could back this up with Latin idioms and quotes from the Talmud.

Once I heard him say to Mother, "What a pity the Jews don't know what an incredible culture they possess. If they knew, they'd cry like children."

When he came to the city, he would stay at our home. The hotel that he loved had gone bankrupt, and he couldn't stand any others. Whenever he had an opportunity to come to town, he'd bring us some precious item from his collection. Mother would scold him, but Uncle Felix argued that no man knew when his time will be up, and that he preferred to distribute his valuables among those he loved and while he was still alive. I was given a lovely antique Italian violin. Uncle Felix had tested my hearing and pronounced, "Excellent hearing. You deserve a violin."

For my part, I promised to practice every day for at least three hours.

EVEN MY UNCLE was not aware of how prescient he was: the situation deteriorated from month to month. At first he fought with the thieves and robbers; when he was told that the robbers were actually in cahoots with the police, he pitted himself against the police. But the moment the official responsible for the region sided with the rabble-rousers, Uncle Felix had no choice but to load a truck with his household belongings and come to the city. He stored his things in our large warehouse and leased out his estate for next to nothing.

Uncle Felix lived near us in a rented apartment and would come see us once a week, sometimes twice. He no longer wore the splendid suits that he used to wear on the estate. Instead, he wore casual clothes that added a charming touch, complementing his silver hair. I never heard him complain or blame anyone. If Aunt Regina was mentioned, a slight cloud would pass across his forehead. Although they were very different, they had been close. It was not without amazement that my mother would point this out.

My uncle transferred most of his art collection to us. The pictures changed the appearance of our house; it began to look a little bit like a museum. My mother was extremely proud of the collection and invited the few friends that we had to come see it.

Uncle Felix kept his equanimity even when life became very hard. A Ukrainian estate landlord, an old acquaintance, wanted to hide him on his estate, but Uncle Felix refused. During the ghetto days, he lived with us in one room. The precious collection was with us, but we didn't know how to save it. Finally, my uncle handed it over to the director of a local bank, who promised to keep it safe until the bad times were over. He came to collect the packages one night, a tall man with large hands. I knew we would never see this treasure again.

Winter came and packed us even more tightly together.

There was no firewood for heating, and no water. Uncle Felix, who had been an officer in the Austrian army, kept his erect bearing even during those dark days.

Afterward, on the deportation march, for the entire length of the long route through the heart of the Ukrainian steppes, Uncle Felix helped to bury people so that they wouldn't become carrion for the birds of prey. He himself died of typhus in a barn, and Father, who wanted to bury him, couldn't find a spade. We laid him upon a pile of hay.

3

IN THE SUMMER OF 1937, my mother and I traveled home on a night train. I don't know why we left our vacation home in the village in such haste. We traveled in luxury, in a first-class compartment that was half empty. Mother read a book, and I leafed through a picture album. The mingled smells of cake and tobacco wafted into the compartment, and it was pleasant to flick through the album and to gaze around. Mother asked me if I was tired, and I said that I wasn't.

After that the lights were dimmed. Mother closed her book and dozed off. For a long time, I listened carefully to the tiny noises that rustled in the car. Then, from a dark end of the car, a tall and buxom waitress suddenly appeared. She squatted right down on her knees, looked at me, and asked what my name was. I told her.

"And how old are you?"

For some reason, this question amused me, but I told her I was five.

"And where are you going?"

"Home."

"A beautiful boy, bound for a beautiful city," she said. Her words didn't make me laugh, and yet I laughed anyway. In the midst of this, she held out her two large palms and said, "Why don't you give me your hand? Wouldn't you like to be my friend?"

I put my hands on her open palms. She kissed them and said, "Beautiful hands." A strange pleasantness flowed through my body.

"Come with me and I'll give you something good," she said, holding me tight as she swung me upward. Her breasts were large and warm, but the height made me dizzy.

At the end of the car, she had a cubicle. The cubicle contained a folding bed, a small dresser, and a closet.

"Come, let's find something nice for you. What would you like?" she asked, and put me down on her folding bed.

"Halvah," I said, for some reason.

"Halvah," she said, quite taken aback. "Only peasant children eat halvah. Children from good homes like the taste of more delicate things."

"What?"

"I'll show you right now," she said. Holding both my feet, she quickly took off my shoes and socks and crammed my toes into her mouth. "Tasty, very tasty," she said.

The touch was pleasant but made me shiver a bit. "Now let's give this handsome young man something very tasty," she said, and took a bar of chocolate out of her little purse. The chocolate—a cheap brand wrapped in simple paper, whose brand name was Healthy and Tasty—was a byword for cheapness and vulgarity in our home.

"Don't you want to taste it?"

"No," I said, and laughed.

"It's very good," she said, taking off the wrapping and showing me the brown bar. "Taste it. I like this chocolate."

"No, thanks."

"So—what chocolate do you like, my spoiled little sweetie?"

"Suchard," I told her truthfully.

"Suchard. That's fancy chocolate—chocolate without taste. Chocolate should be heavy and full of nuts."

She immediately lifted me up again, swung me around, and squeezed me to her large body. "Suchard is chocolate for the rich, but it's chocolate that's finished too quickly. Now, we like lots of chocolate. You see?"

I didn't understand, but I nodded as if I did.

"When does the train stop?" I asked for some reason.

"It's the express. The express stops only at the last stop, and the last stop is Czernowitz," she said, baring her square teeth and continuing to stroke the soles of my feet.

"Nice?" she asked.

"Very," I couldn't help telling her.

"I'll keep you amused until the morning," she said, and laughed. And as she was kneading my body, kissing and pinching me, the door of the tiny room opened, and there stood Mother at the doorway.

"What are you doing here?" Her eyes opened wide.

"Nothing at all; we're playing. Erwin was bored and wanted to play."

"Erwin never gets bored," my mother corrected her.

"You were sleeping and Erwin got bored. One shouldn't let a handsome little boy like Erwin get bored. True?" She turned her face to me. Mother for some reason didn't take her eyes off me. She wasn't angry, but her pinched smile bespoke suspicion.

"Have you been here a long time?" Mother asked. Now I knew that something was amiss. "Let's go," she said, holding out her hand.

"Erwin is a very clever boy," the waitress said, trying to win Mother over.

"But not careful enough." Mother couldn't restrain herself.

"Both wise and careful, I swear to you." The waitress spoke like a peasant woman.

Mother didn't react. She pulled me decisively toward the corridor.

"What did you do?" she asked when we were almost at our seats.

"We talked."

"You should be more careful."

"Why?"

"Because these kinds of people don't know the meaning of boundaries."

The train moved on. The first light of dawn tinted the dark clouds with a rose-pink hue. Mother didn't speak. Her face became more and more closed off from me. There was no doubt now—she was angry.

"Mother."

"What?"

"When are we getting home?"

"In a while."

"And Father will be waiting for us at the station?"

"I expect so."

I wanted to placate her, so I said, "Seven times seven is forty-nine."

On hearing this, she hugged me.

"Next week I'll know the entire multiplication table, I promise."

No one was urging me to learn the table by heart, but I apparently thought that this would make Mother happy.

"But you should be more careful." She hadn't forgotten my sin.

Father was waiting for us at the station. I ran up to him. He tossed me in the air and kissed my cheek.

"How was the trip?" Father asked gently.

"Not bad," said Mother dryly.

"Were there delays?"

"No."

"What more could one ask?" said Father, in the tone he seemed to have adopted of late.

4

NINETEEN THIRTY-EIGHT was a bad year. Rumors were rife, and it became clear that we were trapped. My father sent telegrams to relatives and friends in Uruguay and Chile, he even tried to obtain a visa to America, but it was useless. Nothing went smoothly anymore. People who had previously been welcome in our house, or who were trusted business partners or childhood friends, suddenly behaved as if they didn't know us or were transformed into enemies. Despair lurked everywhere. It was strange, but even then there were the blind optimists in our midst who interpreted every turn of events for the good; they could show, with considerable panache, that the might of Hitler was illusory, and that Germany would eventually return to what it had been before. They argued that it was only a question of time. Feeling that the ground was burning beneath our feet, Father knocked on every possible door.

In the spring, we learned that Grandfather, my mother's father, had contracted a fatal illness, and that his days were numbered. Grandfather took it calmly. His moonlike gaze seemed only to grow more owlish and penetrating.

One night he told my mother, "This separation between the living and the dead is an illusion. The transition is so much easier than people suppose. It's only a change of place, going up a level."

On hearing that, my mother cried like a baby.

GRANDFATHER'S DAILY ROUTINE was not altered in the least. In the morning, he'd leave for prayers, and on his return from the synagogue, he'd have a bite to eat, sitting on the veranda. For him, sitting out on the veranda was a sort of preparation for his daily study. Sometimes he would keep the same book next to him for many days, and sometimes he'd change it, but there would never be more than one book on his table at a time.

Father rushed from place to place, and when he came back in the evening, his face would be somber. My mother tried to please him by making his favorite dishes. After the meal, he'd sit on the sofa, his eyes closed, drowning within himself.

Death hovered everywhere, but not in Grandfather's room. There, the windows would be open and the curtains would waft in the breeze. From time to time, my mother brought him a glass of tea with lemon. Grandfather would thank her and ask her about something, and my mother would sit by him. It was easy to see that he loved his daughter, and that having her near him made him happy.

Everyone attempted to hide the state of his health from Grandfather. They also tried to hide what was going on around us. But Grandfather knew everything, and he didn't allow confusion or muddle to govern him. He spoke of death just as he used to speak of any long journey he was about to take. When Grandmother was alive, she would try to get him to pack another coat or another sweater, but Grandfather loved light suitcases, and that was his argument now as well: The road isn't long, and there is nothing to fear.

Once a day I would go in to see him. He would stroke my head, show me the letters in the book he was studying, and tell me a short story, a fable, or a parable. Once he told me one that I could not understand. When he saw that I had not understood it, he said, "Not important, the main thing is to appreciate this morning." Even this was beyond my understanding. Nonetheless, it has remained with me to this day, like a pleasant riddle. Sometimes it seems to me that Grandfather didn't belong with us, but had come to visit from other regions—he was so different.

That spring, he was still living in the village where he, his father, and his father's father had been born. Initially, he had refused to abandon his farm, but when his condition deteriorated and he needed hospital treatment, he agreed to come to the city. My mother cleared out a room for him and went to fetch him in a carriage. And so he came to us.

From the moment of his arrival, Mother changed completely. Her face grew longer; she now made her way frequently and anxiously from the kitchen to his room. Grandfather asked for nothing, but Mother knew exactly what he needed. When Mother served him plum compote, his face would light up for a moment. It had always been one of his favorite dishes.

In the morning, he'd stir, get up, and go out to pray. His faith was apparently stronger than his body, which was weakening. Mother often tried to persuade him not to go to the early-morning prayers in the synagogue. But he would not agree, not even for her; going to these prayers seemed to summon fresh reserves of strength from his body. He'd return full of wonder.

Sometimes he'd be overcome by longing for his village.

His longing was tangible, as if it brought him close to the trees and to the streams that surrounded his home. Now his house was all locked up, and two peasants were taking care of his fruit trees and vegetable garden. The poultry and other farm animals had long since been sold, apart from one cow that Grandfather had requested be kept. Once I heard him tell Mother, "Take me back to the village, please; it's hard for me to be away from my home."

Mother hesitated for a moment. "Let's see what the doctors have to say," she said.

In the evening, Dr. Feldman came by and persuaded Grandfather that in his condition it would be best for him to stay near the hospital, and not in a village some fifty kilometers from the city. Grandfather listened and said, "It seems that this is how it has to be."

Our home was without Torah and without religious observance, but from the time of Grandfather's arrival, it changed radically. Mother made the kitchen completely kosher, and we would eat only vegetarian food; we wouldn't light a fire on the Sabbath, and when Father wanted to smoke on the Sabbath, he would go out behind the house or into a nearby street.

Victoria, our elderly maid, treated Grandfather with enormous respect. Once a day she scrubbed the floor of his room. I heard her say to Mother, "Not everyone has the good fortune to have a father like your father. He's a really holy man."

Victoria could say things that made me afraid. Once she said, "The Jews have forgotten that there's a God in heaven."

"Not all of them," my mother protested, trying to soften her words.

"In the synagogue there's barely a quorum in the mornings." Victoria stood her ground.

I had no doubt there was a God in heaven, who governed not only the stars in the sky but His creatures as well. I acquired this belief from another servant, who filled in for Victoria for a short time. Younger than Victoria and extremely pretty, Anna-Maria would repeatedly tell me in secret that there's a God in heaven and He governs not only His stars but all His creatures as well.

In the afternoons, Grandfather would get up from his bed and go out on the veranda. Grandfather did not speak of his beliefs, but all his actions were directed toward those beliefs. Sometimes it seemed to me that he was lonely because he wasn't understood, but at other times I felt that his room was full of vitality—full of invisible guests who came to visit him and with whom he communicated in the language of silence.

Father and Mother sometimes quarreled in the kitchen, arguing with their hands clenched, trying to convince each other with a flood of words. When the words led nowhere, they moved away from each other and fell silent. But Grandfather's silence was void of anger and was more like a heavy pillow onto which one could lay one's head. When Grandfather came to live with us, Father stopped criticizing Jews and their religious beliefs. He became withdrawn, spoke very little, and on his return from the exhausting attempts to get us transit papers, he would come straight into the kitchen, where Mother would pour him a cup of coffee and spread two slices of bread with fruit preserves. He would eat distractedly and rapidly, finishing the two slices in an instant.

This was the atmosphere at home during that year: Grandfather's calm and Father's tumult. From time to time, and usually at night, Father would take me outside, and we would wander for hours. He loved the quiet cobbled streets at night. He would stride down street after street, with me trot-

ting behind him. Sometimes he would stop and say something: a sentence or a few words. I'm not sure to whom his
words were addressed. Sometimes there rose from within him
a kind of unexpected, strange happiness, and he might begin
to sing out loud. And that's how we would reach the river.
Father loved the river, and on more than one occasion, I saw
him bend down toward it. Once he said to me, "Water is
closer to us than the earth," and he laughed, as if he had put
some nonsense into words. These hasty outings were not
always pleasant, but I recall them more vividly than the
houses that I used to visit.

I could not know that these were the last days we were
to spend at home, and yet I was constantly telling myself that
I needed to sit next to Grandfather and watch him. I felt I
should not lose sight of him sitting on the veranda, or of how
he looked when engrossed in a book. Mother, too, sitting next
to him, must not be forgotten. I felt that the coming days
would not be good ones, but no one could have imagined the
tidal wave that was already surging toward us with full force.
I'd lie in bed for hours, reading Jules Verne, playing chess with
myself, and feeling sorry that Father was so distracted—not
shaving in the morning, and leaving the house in haste.

Sometimes it seemed to me that Father was trying to
burrow a tunnel through which he wanted to save us, but that
the tunneling was proceeding so slowly that it was doubtful he
would be able to finish it in time. At the same time, he was
trying to find us berths on a ship that would take us to Gibral-
tar. Each day was a desperate attempt to break through the
ring that was tightening around us. Mother, however, was so
caught up in Grandfather's illness that Father's words—or,
more correctly, his plans—left absolutely no impression on
her. To her lack of attentiveness and her absentmindedness
Father reacted with nervous shrugging of his shoulders; harsh

words were exchanged, and they brought up the names of people or places of which I hadn't heard.

Death surrounded us on every side, yet Father seemed to think that if we tried hard enough there could be some respite, or even perhaps rescue. "We mustn't give up," he would say. It was hard to know to what exactly he was referring, but he invariably directed his most severe criticism at himself, and hardly ever at us. Once I heard him say to Grandfather, "We need divine mercy, abundant mercy." I wondered how such a phrase could come from his mouth, and it seemed to me that Grandfather was also taken aback. So many incomprehensible sentences were whispered at home. It seemed that we were living in the midst of a searing riddle.

Mother sometimes waved her hand, as though trying to dispel bad spirits. For some reason these gestures angered Father, and he said that what they needed now was a cool head, not despair. Yet despair confronted us. For a moment Mother rallied, and then it seemed to me that once again she might burst into tears.

At the end of the summer, on a clear and absolutely cloudless day, Grandfather dozed off and never awoke from his sleep. Victoria noticed that he had ceased breathing and rushed to get Mother. Mother fell on her knees without uttering a sound. When she noticed me in the doorway, she grabbed hold of me and said, "What are you doing here?" She immediately took me to our elderly neighbor, Mrs. Horowitz. I didn't want to go, and I threw a tantrum. My screaming must have only made my mother more determined, because she then slapped my face. Mrs. Horowitz held out a piece of candy wrapped in golden foil and said, "Don't cry, child."

I lay there, drumming my legs on the ground, overwhelmed by anger and humiliation. Late that night, tired and confused, I was brought back home.

The house had changed beyond recognition. It was filled with people. Victoria was serving coffee in small cups, and the living room was full of smoke. Father stood apart. He wore a *kippah* on his head, and his body was swaying like a drunkard's. Mother sat on the floor wrapped in a blanket, surrounded by unfamiliar people. People talked not about Grandfather's death, but about practical matters; perhaps they did so to divert Mother's attention, but Mother would not be diverted. Her eyes were large and wide open.

Suddenly it seemed to me that everyone was pleased that death had gone away, that now it was possible just to sit and drink the coffee that Victoria was serving. This sense of things going on as if nothing had happened hurt me, and I fled to my room. To my surprise, even my room was full of people.

This time, Father did not hold back. Then and there, in front of everyone, he derided what he called the tribal burial customs that did not respect the dead and that lacked all good taste. In particular he blasted the Burial Society for rushing through the prayers and for being in such a hurry to hand out spades to the mourners—and then demanding donations on top of their fee. I knew that he didn't approve of Jewish burial customs, but this time he vented his anger and held nothing back. He concluded his tirade by saying, "I, at any rate, will not abandon my body to them. Better to be interred in a lepers' graveyard than to be buried in a Jewish cemetery."

People dispersed soon after this, and Father's voice echoed in the empty house. I didn't know if Mother agreed with his words. She sat on the floor, and not a sound issued from her mouth. In the way she sat there was something of Grandfather. Perhaps in the way she rested her hand on her knees.

5

IN THE GHETTO, children and madmen were friends. All the social frameworks had collapsed: there was no school, no homework, no getting up early in the morning, and no putting out the lights at night. We'd play in the courtyards, on the staircases, between trees, and in all kinds of gloomy corners. Sometimes the madmen would join in our games. The new chaos worked to their advantage as well. The Mental Institution and the Hospital for the Mentally Ill had been closed down, and people who'd been let out of those places wandered through the streets, smiling aimlessly. Their smiles also carried more than a trace of gloating, as if to say, "All these years you laughed at us for mixing things up, confusing things, confusing time; we weren't precise, we called places and things by strange names. But now it's clear that we were right. You didn't believe us, you were all so damned self-righteous that you thought us completely worthless. You packed us off to institutions and you shut us away behind lock and key." There was something frightening in the gaiety of their smiles.

They celebrated their freedom in strange ways. In the park they would lie stretched out on their backs, singing, and the young men among them would call out compliments to girls and young women. But most of the time they would sit on the benches in the public parks and smile. They treated children as their equals. They would sit cross-legged and play five stones, dominoes, and chess. They would play catch, and even football. Anxious parents, at their wits' end, would swoop down on them. The insane learned to spot the parents early and would run away in time.

There were some dangerous ones, too, among the insane—madmen who'd menace us with real fury. We children also learned to spot them coming, and we'd run away. But most of them were quiet and polite and would make sense when they spoke. There were even those who you would never think were insane—ones you could question about math, geography, or a book by Jules Verne. Also among the insane were doctors, lawyers, and rich people; and there were some whose property, as soon as they'd been institutionalized, was appropriated by their children. Occasionally an insane man would stop a game to tell us about his wife and children. Some of them were religiously observant and would pray, make a blessing before eating something, or try to teach us the morning or the evening prayers.

I liked looking at them. Their faces were expressive. They enjoyed playing, but didn't know how to win. We were better at it than they were. When they lost, they'd burst out laughing and say, "Even the tiniest tots are better than we are." True, there were those who became infuriated when they lost and might overturn the board or throw things around. But there weren't too many of these. Most of them accepted defeat graciously and even smilingly.

Occasionally one of the insane would lose control, raging wildly in the street, thrashing out, or biting. Right away the ghetto police would be called in. They would waste no time and round them all up. After a day or two behind bars, they would again be released. And right away we would invite them to play chess or dominoes. It was strange how they harbored no resentment, neither for the police nor for those who'd handed them over.

I liked to observe their gestures—the way they held a plate, or tore off chunks of bread. Sometimes they'd fall asleep in the park, all crumpled up, as if they weren't grown-up people but children who had suddenly got tired in the middle of a game. During the days of the deportation, they tried to escape, to hide, but the police, of course, were sharper than they were. In their great naïveté, the insane would hide under the benches in the park, or climb up trees. It wasn't hard to catch them; even the way they ran was clumsy and awkward. The ghetto police would grab them roughly and load them onto the trucks. No one interceded on their behalf—it was as if there was a general consensus that if we all had to be deported, then they should be the first. Even their own families didn't try to save them.

During one of the deportations, I saw a truck filled with the insane. People threw them slices of bread, chunks of pie, and baked potatoes. They jumped to catch the food while it was still in the air, but quite hopelessly. They stood next to the grille of the truck and smiled, as if to say, "We never managed to do the right thing, and because of it we weren't loved. But now, when we are being taken away from you, why are you casting us away with this hail of food? We don't need your food now. A little attention, a little love would have gone a long way. Instead of this, you're fobbing us off, tossing us this tasteless food."

With that expression on their faces, they left us forever.

6

EVERY TOWN, it would seem, had its own Janusz Korczak.
In our town the person who led the blind children to the railway station was the director of the Institute for the Blind, the
teacher Gustav Gotesman. He was short, the same height as
the children, and he did everything fast. He was renowned for
his method of teaching: everything was learned through
music. Melodies were continually wafting from the Institute
for the Blind. Gotesman believed that music not only served
as a good instrument for learning but also enhanced sensitivity in people. All the children at the institute spoke in
melodic tones, even when they addressed one another; the
frailty of their little bodies complemented the pleasantness of
their speech. In the afternoons, they would sit on the steps
and sing. They sang classical songs and Yiddish folk songs.
Their voices had harmony and sweetness, and passersby
would stand by the railings and listen to them.

Gustav Gotesman was a well-known communist, and
he had been arrested on more than one occasion. When he

was arrested, his deputy, also a short man and a communist, would take his place. Were it not for his utter devotion, the institute's board of governors would have fired him. The respectable tradesmen who sat on the board claimed that Gustav was teaching the children communism, that his influence on them was detrimental, and that when they grew up they would disseminate the poison they were imbibing. However, the more canny tradesmen on the board had no such misgivings; they claimed that it wasn't important what Gotesman was teaching—what mattered was his complete dedication. They argued that communists who were blind from birth presented no danger; on the contrary, communist dogmas would sound ridiculous in their mouths.

The bickering among the members of the board did not abate. One of the tradesmen, whose contribution amounted to half the institute's budget, was a religious man. He set two conditions: religious studies and Sabbath observance in the institute. The argument continued for some time. Eventually a compromise was reached: religious studies twice a week, and prayer on the Sabbath eve.

The religious-studies teacher who was brought in to the institute was the son of the Rabbi of Zjadov. He duly came twice a week to teach the children Hebrew and Torah; on Friday night he led the prayers. The children loved his teaching and the prayers. It was not long before the Sabbath-eve prayer became famous throughout the town. People would gather by the railings and listen with wonder.

Gustav Gotesman did not give up. He claimed that the children's prayer was not prayer but song, and that music, not religious beliefs, directed the course of their lives. He said that the time when religion held sway had long passed, and that now there was only the belief in man, in his capacity to change, to build a just society, and to sacrifice himself for others. It was this belief that he would drum into the children day and night, and instead of the prayer "Hear, O Israel," which they should have said every night, he composed a song that was called "Hear, O Man," in which man was called upon to give of himself to whoever needed him. Like every believer, Gotesman was also a fanatic. He waged his war against the son of the Rabbi of Zjadov using all the means at his disposal. However, there was one thing that he was forbidden to do, and that was to preach that religion was the opiate of the people. Still, although he was indeed prevented from declaring this in public, in private he whispered whatever he whispered.

The struggle came to an end in 1941. Overnight, the Institute for the Blind, which was in the poor area of town, became the very center of the ghetto. Songs were constantly bursting forth from its windows, and the melodies spread out over the ghetto, wafting over its persecuted residents till darkness.

No one knew what the next day would bring, but the blind children apparently knew more than we did. They guessed that the future wasn't too bright. One of their songs was sung again and again each evening: "Death Should Die." In time, it became the institute's anthem. It was a song with a firm rhythm, and it sounded like a defiant elegy.

Gotesman worked day and night with the children. Most of his lessons were in music, but in the intervals he would drum his beliefs into them: the extreme conditions in which we find ourselves must not destroy our belief in people; we must help the weak even if it means sharing our last crust of bread with them; true communism means not only a more equitable division of wealth but also giving with all one's heart.

On October 13, 1942, the director of the Institute for the Blind was ordered to bring his children to the railway station. The children dressed in their Sabbath best; each put a book in Braille in his backpack, along with a plate, a mug, a fork, a spoon, and a change of clothes. Gotesman explained to them that the road to the railway station was not a long one, and that they would make five brief stops en route. At these stops they would sing classical songs and Yiddish songs. When they reached the railway station, they would sing their anthem. The children were excited, but not frightened. Their eyes widened with anticipation. They understood that from now on they would be called upon to do things that had not yet been required of them.

The first stop was the Emperor's Well. It was famous in the town for its excellent water. Orthodox Jews, however, did not use it, since it was used by all the townsfolk, and the owner of the inn and the non-Jewish butcher would draw from it. At this first stop, the children sang songs by Schubert. There was a strong wind near the well, and the children strained to raise their voices. No one was there apart from them, and their song sounded like a prayer. Gotesman was usually careful not to criticize the children outside the confines of the institute. This time, however, he contravened his own rules and said, "The song is sacred, and even under trying conditions, none of its notes should be overlooked."

At the second stop, in Labor Square, there was also no one waiting for them. The children sang a song from Bach, and Gotesman was satisfied with their rendering. It was at this square, on the first day of May, that Jewish communists would gather. The assembly never lasted more than a few minutes, for the police would spring out, swinging their clubs at the demonstrators to disperse them. This time, however, there was not a soul in the square, except for some Ukrainian youths who had climbed the trees that surrounded it and threw stones as they shouted, "Jews to the cattle cars!"

At the third stop, women brought the children water and slices of bread spread with oil. The children were happy with this warm reception and sang Yiddish songs. When they finished singing, the women didn't want to let them go. "We won't give you our children!" they shouted. Gotesman intervened and said, "We'll go along with everyone else. We are no different from anyone. Whatever happens to everyone will happen to us as well." One woman could not restrain herself and yelled, "Communist!"

At the fourth stop, next to the ghetto's fence, many emotional people were waiting for them and showered them with gifts. One man on a balcony shouted at the top of his voice, "We love you, children, and soon we'll meet again. We'll never, ever forget how you sang. You were the angelic choirboys of our ghetto."

By turns, the children sang classical songs and folk songs. Even part of a Verdi opera. Here, too, women surrounded the children and didn't allow them to continue on their way. But now they were no longer on their own. The soldiers posted alongside the ghetto's fence began swinging their clubs, and all at once, the singing ceased.

On the narrow road to the railway station, the children halted and again broke into song. The guards must have been taken by surprise and let them sing at first, but not for long. They immediately set upon the children with their clubs, and the children, who were holding one another's hands, trembled as one body. "Don't be afraid, children," Gotesman whispered, and they managed to overcome their pain. At the railway station, they still managed to sing their anthem in its entirety before being pushed into the cattle cars.

7

I MET WONDERFUL PEOPLE during the long years of the war. In a way, it was a pity that it went by in such a blur, and that I was only a child. During the war, children were ignored. Children were like the straw on which everyone trod. But there were some remarkable people who, amid the great confusion, comforted an abandoned child, gave him a slice of bread, or threw a coat around him.

On the way to the Ukraine, at a railway station filled with people being deported, I saw a woman taking care of an abandoned child. He must have been about four years old. The child had a full head of hair, and the woman was sitting on some luggage and combing his hair out with long, slow strokes, as if they were in a public park and not a chaotic station. The child's pale face was full of wonder; he seemed to understand that this was a special act of kindness that happens but once in a lifetime.

In the evening, a large freight train pulled into the station, and the doors gaped open. Ukrainian soldiers were lashing about with their whips, and there was tremendous confusion. The woman, who must have known what was awaiting us, urged the child to run away. She showed him a passageway under the stairs, but the child clung to her legs and pleaded, "I don't want to." When she tried to drag him, he whispered, "I'm afraid."

"You mustn't be afraid," said the woman, raising her voice.

"I'm afraid," the child repeated, as if asking that she take his words into her heart.

"But you mustn't be afraid," she repeated in a sharp voice.

When he heard her tone, the boy's whole body seemed to shrink.

"I'm angry with you!" The woman stood up, forcibly pulling at the child's small arms. But the child clung to her ankles without moving.

"If you don't run away, I'll give you a thrashing!" she threatened. This only made the child clutch even harder at her ankles.

"Get out of here! Go!" She changed her tone, speaking to him as if he weren't a child but a puppy dog.

The child resisted even more.

"I'll beat you," she said, and pulled at one of her legs. But the child's grasp must have been strong. There were people shoving at the woman from all sides, and she, in sheer despair, raised her voice and shouted, "Take him from me! I can't stand it any longer!"

No one paid any attention to her or to her shouts. Everyone was being pushed into the the freight cars, which looked too narrow to contain so many people. Eventually someone trod on the child's body, and he slid off her legs. This must have given the woman some relief, for she lifted up her bundle and was borne off by those pushing straight into an open car. The child was swallowed up by all the legs.

"Tina!" A child's voice could suddenly be heard, distinct from all the others.

"What do you want?" The woman raised her voice so that it would be heard.

"Tina!" the child repeated, with unmistakable pleading.

The woman threw away the bundle. With an abrupt movement she managed to extricate herself from the press of people pushing and shoving and to return to the spot from which she had been pushed.

"Where are you?" she called, searching for the child on the ground.

Finally, she found him. He was lying on the ground, bleeding. She bent down and pulled him into a corner that was somewhat sheltered from the whipping and lashing.

She bent down to him, wiped his bleeding face with her dress, and said in a whisper, "What did you do?" The child opened his eyes wide. "I have to go. What can I do? You have to understand this."

The pressure and the noise intensified, and the woman made one final attempt, shouting out her instructions. "Go right to the passageway under the stairs. It will take you from the platform straight out to the fields. Don't tell anyone that you're Jewish. You hear? Get up, now—do you hear me?"

One could see that the child had understood, but apparently he didn't have the strength to move.

"Run! Get out of here!" she urged him.

But there was no reaction from the child, so she took hold of him and lifted him up. In a voice that did not seem to be her own, the woman shouted, "Clear the way, there's an injured child here!"

The pressure was great, and no one paid any attention to her, but, overcome by a force far greater than her own, the woman was pushed straight into one of the freight cars and was immediately swallowed up.

8

MORE THAN FIFTY YEARS have passed since the end of the war. I have forgotten much, even things that were very close to me—places in particular, dates, and the names of people—and yet I can still sense those days in every part of my body. Whenever it rains, it's cold, or a fierce wind is blowing, I am taken back to the ghetto, to the camp, or to the forests where I spent many days. Memory, it seems, has deep roots in the body. Sometimes just the smell of rotting straw, or the sharp call of a bird, is enough to take me back, piercing me deep inside.

I say inside, although I still haven't found the words to give voice to those intense scars on my memory. Over the years I tried, on more than one occasion, to go back and touch the planks on which we slept in the camp, and to taste the watery soup that was doled out there. But all this effort yielded no more than jumbled phrases, incorrect words, disjointed rhythm, weak or exaggerated characters. Profound experience, I've already learned, is easily distorted. This time, too, I won't attempt to put my hand into this fire. It's not what happened in the camp that I'll be recounting, but what happened to those who escaped from it, as I did in the autumn of 1942, when I was ten years old.

I don't remember entering the forest, but I do remember the moment when I stood before a tree laden with red apples. I was so astonished that I took a few steps back. More than my conscious mind does, my body seems to remember those steps backward. If ever I make a wrong movement, or unexpectedly stumble backward, I see the tree with the red apples. It had been two days since any food had passed my lips, and here was a tree full of apples. I could have put out my hand and picked them, but I just stood in wonderment, and the longer I stood there, the deeper the silence that took root in me.

Finally, I sat down and ate a small apple that was on the ground and was partially rotten. After I had eaten it, I must have fallen asleep. When I awoke, the sky had already turned dusky. I didn't know what to do, so I got up on my knees. This position, too, on my knees, I feel to this very day. Any time I'm kneeling, I remember the sunset that was glowing through the trees and I feel happy.

It was only on the following day that I picked an apple from the tree. It was hard and sour, and biting it hurt my teeth, but I kept on chewing, and the pulp went down my constricted throat.

After a few days without food, one's hunger becomes dulled. I didn't stir from that place. It seemed to me that I shouldn't leave the apple tree or the ditch alongside it. But thirst drove me on, and I went to look for water. For an entire day I searched, and only toward evening did I find a stream. I knelt down and drank. The water opened my eyes, and I saw my mother, whom I hadn't been able to visualize for many days. First I saw her standing by the window and gazing out of it, as she used to. But then she suddenly turned to me, wondering how I came to be alone in the forest. I walked toward her, but I immediately understood that if I went too far I'd lose sight of the stream, and so I stopped. I returned to the stream and looked into the same beam of light through which Mother had been revealed to me, but it was closed.

My mother was murdered at the beginning of the war. I didn't see her die, but I did hear her one and only scream. Her death is deep inside me, but more a part of me than her death is her reappearance after it. Any time I'm happy or sad I see her face. She's either leaning on the windowsill or standing at the doorway of our house, as if she's about to come toward me. Now I am thirty years older than she was when she died. Time hasn't added years to her. She's always young and fresh.

The fear that I'd lose the stream was unfounded. I followed it for its entire length, and fortunately it continued right up to the edge of the forest. This was a brook like those I remembered from vacations with my parents, shaded by willow branches and flowing very slowly. Every few hours I'd kneel down and drink from its water. I hadn't learned to pray, but this kneeling brought vividly to mind the peasants who worked the fields and who would drop to their knees, silently crossing themselves.

In a forest no one dies of hunger. Here was a thicket of blueberries, and alongside the trunk of a tree, a strawberry patch. I even found a pear tree. If not for the cold at night, I would have slept more. At that time, I still didn't have a clear notion of death. I'd already seen many dead people in the ghetto and in the camp, and I knew that a dead person doesn't get back up on his feet and is eventually put in a pit. Yet I still didn't grasp death as an end. I continued to expect my parents to come and collect me. This expectation, this tense waiting, stayed with me throughout the war, and it would return to overcome me whenever despair sunk its talons into me.

How many days was I in the forest? Perhaps till it started to rain. Living among the trees, I began to get colder as the days passed. There was no place to hide, and the wetness penetrated my flimsy clothes. Fortunately, I had been wearing little laced boots that my mother had bought me some days before the German invasion, but they had also begun to take on water and become heavy. So I had no choice but to try to find refuge in one of the peasant homes that were scattered over the ridge of the hill next to the forest. As it turned out, they were a considerable distance away. After a long walk, I stood before a hut whose roof was covered with a thick layer of straw. When I drew near the gate, some dogs sprang at me, and I only just managed to run away from them.

On rainy days, peasants don't leave their huts. I stood in the rain, and I knew that it wouldn't be long before I fell into one of the muddy ditches and disappeared. The thought that I might never see my parents again made my knees buckle, and I fell down upon them.

As despair gripped my body, I saw a low house on a neighboring hillside, and I immediately noticed that there were no dogs around it. I knocked on the door and waited in great fear. After a few moments, the door opened and a young woman stood in the doorway.

"What do you want, child?"

"I want to work," I said.

She looked me up and down.

"Come in."

She looked like a peasant woman, yet somehow different. She was wearing a green blouse with shell buttons. I spoke Ukrainian, which was the mother tongue of our maid, Victoria. I had loved her and her language. It didn't surprise me that this woman reminded me of Victoria, even though there was no physical resemblance between them.

"What are you doing here?" she asked.

Instinct whispered to me not to reveal the truth, so I told her that I had been born in a place called Lutshintz, that my parents had been killed in an air raid, and that since then I had been wandering around. She stared at me, and for a moment it seemed as though she was about to grab my coat and slap my face. I was surprised that she didn't.

"You're not a thief?" she asked, with a penetrating look.

"No," I said.

And so I came to stay with her. I did not know who she was or what my work would be. It was raining heavily, and I was just happy to be surrounded by walls, near a hearth that radiated warmth. The windows were small and were covered with bright peasant drapes. On the walls were many pictures cut out of magazines.

By the following day, I had already swept the house, washed the dishes, and peeled potatoes and beets. From then on, I would rise early and work till late at night.

Once a week I'd go to the village store to buy sugar, salt, sausage, and vodka for her. The walk from the hut to the store took an hour and a half. The path was green and filled with tall trees, and cattle grazed there.

Only two years before, I had had parents. Now my existence was no more than what I saw before me. Sometimes I managed to steal some moments for myself, and I would go and sit on the bank of a brook. From there my previous life seemed so far away, it was as if it had never been. Only at night, in my sleep, would I be next to my mother and father, in the yard or on the street. Awakening in the morning was a blow, like a slap in the face.

The woman was called Maria, and she wasn't married. Almost every night a different man would come into the hut, and they would shut themselves away together behind a curtain. At first they would talk and drink vodka, and afterward there'd be loud laughter and, in the end, silence. This sequence would repeat itself night after night. "Don't be frightened," I would say to myself, and yet I was. Along with the fear, sometimes there was a strange pleasure.

The night did not always end quietly. Occasionally an argument broke out. Maria didn't mince her words; when she did not like something or thought that someone might be cheating her, she shouted in an awful, blood-curdling voice that could make the walls of the hut shudder. And if this wasn't enough, she might also throw a plate, a shoe, or any other object that she could lay her hands on. But there were also nights that ended quietly, in kisses. The man would declare his love and promise to bring many presents, and Maria, for her part, laughed and teased.

Maria's hut was one long room that was curtained off at one end. I would sit on the huge stove and eavesdrop. Sometimes I could not restrain myself and would peek through the cracks of the planks above the stove. I would usually be too frightened to see anything, but once I glimpsed Maria and she was completely naked. A warm pleasure washed over me.

Sometimes she would tell me to go outside and pick wildflowers. After picking them, I would fill jugs with water and thrust the stalks into them. Once, during a moment of fury, she grabbed one of the jugs and threw it right at the head of the tall peasant who was growling at her from deep in his throat, like a bear.

Maria knew no fear. When something did not please her, or when a man did not behave properly, she would hurl a stream of curses at him. If the man failed to apologize, or if the apology seemed inadequate, she would fling some object at him or throw him out of the hut. "You witch!" I heard a man shout at her on more than one occasion.

She had three wooden tubs in her hut. In the smallest

she washed her feet: in the medium one she would wash her body after a client had left; and the third one, the largest, was the bathtub where she would pamper herself. She would soak herself in it for hours on end, singing, chattering away, reminiscing, or even confessing. More than once I observed her lounging in the large tub, submerged in the water, a long, lazy creature that even the large tub could not contain.

Suddenly it was winter, and the men no longer came as before. Maria would sit by the table shuffling cards. Playing with them amused her. Sometimes she would burst out laughing, but at other times her face would suddenly darken and she would let out a shriek. Once, during one of her black moments, when the sandwich that I'd served her was not to her liking, she grabbed me and shouted, "You wretch, I'll kill you!"

But she wasn't always angry. Her moods could change like the skies. As soon as the clouds lifted from her face, she would be full of joy. More than once, she picked me up in her arms. She was not particularly large, but she was extremely strong. With just her shoulder, she could shove the cow in the barn. Most of the time she was engrossed in herself and did not talk to me. It seemed to me then that she was dreaming of someplace else.

During one of the long winter nights, she told me that she had family in the distant city of Kishinev, and that one day she planned to travel there to visit them. I wanted to ask her when, but I didn't. I had already learned that it was best not to ask. Questions made her angry, and I'd already been given slaps for my questions. I tried to make myself scarce and to ask as little as possible.

In the winter she slept late or lounged in bed. I would serve her a mug of coffee and a slab of bread spread with butter, and she would eat it propped up against the pillows. She seemed younger. She sang a lot, cut out flowers from paper, baked a cake, or sat by the mirror for hours, combing her hair.

"And did you have brothers and sisters?" she asked, to my surprise.

"No."

"Better that way. I have two sisters, but I'm not close to them. They're married, and they have grown children. Even my parents don't love me," she said, smiling to herself. But usually she paid no attention to me. Deep in her own thoughts, mumbling to herself, she dredged up the names of people and places and cursed. Her cursing was bitter and even more frightening than when she screamed and shouted.

By the time winter set in, my arms had grown stronger. Food was not plentiful, but at night I would climb down and steal a slice of sausage or a sliver of halvah, leftovers from the meals that Maria had prepared for her guests. Now I could easily draw the bucket up from the well and carry it straight back to the house. My former life seemed distant and blurred to me. Sometimes a word, a sentence, or a glimpse of memory from home would overcome me unexpectedly and stir me deeply.

During one of my shopping expeditions to the village, a Ukrainian child latched on to me, shouting "Jew-boy!"

I froze.

The fear that someone would identify me had loomed over me ever since I had left the camp, and with this child's shout my fears were realized.

Instinct prompted me to react, and so I ran after the boy. Taken aback by my daring, he started to shout, "Help! Help!" and disappeared into one of the yards. I was satisfied with my reaction, but in my heart I took this as a warning: there must still be something, some trait, that was giving me away.

From then on, I took care to cover up any signs that might betray me. In the toolshed I found an old, worn-out vest, and I asked Maria for permission to wear it. I also found a pair of peasant shoes, which I bound with rope, as the peasants did. Strangely, the threadbare old clothes infused me with new strength.

Toward the end of the winter, I realized I had grown taller. It was a very small change, but I could feel it. The palms of my hands had become broader and harder. I became friendly with the cow, and I learned how to milk her. Even more important, I was no longer afraid of dogs. I adopted two puppies, and whenever I returned from the village they would come out to greet me with yelps of affection.

The puppies were my good friends. I occasionally spoke to them in my mother tongue and told them about my parents and my house. The words that came out of my mouth sounded so strange to me that I thought I must be lying to them. One night Maria surprised me with a question about my family's origins. Without the slightest hesitation I answered, "Ukrainian. Son of Ukrainians," and I was happy with the way the reply had come out of me. I went back to sleep, but not without registering a warning: What had made her ask?

I got used to this new life and could even say that I liked it. I loved the cow, the puppies, the bread that Maria baked in the oven, the yogurt in the clay bowl, and I even loved the hard household chores. One time Maria shut herself behind her curtain and cried and cried. I had no idea why, and I did not dare ask her. Her life, it appears, was entangled in the lives of many people. Sometimes she'd get scraps of greetings from her elderly parents and from her sisters. Even her ex-husband continued to bother her from a distance. She was persecuted perhaps even more than I was, but she didn't give in. She fought her enemies with all her might. Most of all, she fought with herself and with the demons that surrounded her.

She would repeatedly claim that there were demons popping up everywhere, and you needed eyes on the back of your head to see them. To drown her troubles, Maria drank vodka incessantly. Men lusted after her flesh, and their bites on her neck and shoulders were visible to the eye. She would curse those who bit, calling them "swine," but not without pride at having driven them crazy with lust.

The vodka, the men, and the ranting would tire her out, and then she would sleep in, sometimes till late in the afternoon. Sleep did her good. She would get out of bed light and youthful and would start to hum. I would serve her a mug of coffee, and she would call me her "foolish lambkin," for my hair was curly then. Sometimes she would give my bottom an affectionate pinch. I loved her good moods, and I was afraid of her depressions. When she was happy, she would sing, dance, call out the name of Jesus, and say, "My beloved Saviour won't ever betray me."

Maria's happy spells would fill the hut with a wonderful light, but her depressions were more powerful than her happiness. They were deep and lingering, and they could instantly darken the hut. In one of her black moods she shouted at me, "Bastard, son of bastards! Liar, son of liars! I'll cut your throat with a kitchen knife!"

This threat, more than any other, bit into my soul. It was clear: she knew my secret, and when the time came, she would carry out her threat. Were it not for the snow, I would have run away, but even though it was not falling quite as heavily as it had been, it still fell day and night, and it darkened the days.

Eventually the snowfalls ceased and the rains began. My life emptied of all memory and became as smooth as the slopes of the pasture that surrounded me. Even in my dreams I no longer saw my parents. Sometimes it seemed to me that I had been born in this darkness, that what had existed before had been just an illusion. Once I dreamed that I saw my mother, and it seemed as though she saw me but then turned her back on me. This hurt me so much that the next day I vented my anger on the poor beast in the cowshed.

The end of winter came, but it did not warm my body. The path from the hut to the village had turned into a sticky mire. I would return home totally covered in mud. For some reason, the young men whom Maria loved did not come. In their place came the elderly peasants, heavy and silent, whom Maria called "the old cart horses." She would lie with them grudgingly and stand her ground relentlessly in the bargaining that followed. Once she struggled with one of them and really scratched him good and proper.

The days became clearer, but they brought me no peace. I was afraid of Maria. She would down bottle after bottle, curse, and throw things. Even at me. If the sausage or the vodka was not to her liking, she would scratch my face, call me "bastard of bastards," and hurl curses at me.

What I feared came to pass, but not as I had imagined. The fierce winds that had beaten against the hut for more than a month eventually brought down the roof and the walls. Apparently the old wooden hut was already rotted through, and it collapsed under the onslaught of the winds. Suddenly, in broad daylight, there we stood, Maria and I, in the midst of the gaping hut. The household objects, and the bed upon which so many peasants had kneaded Maria's flesh, had been tossed out with one violent gust, as if flung upward. A heavy beam lay across the large quilt that Maria used to wrap herself in.

At the sight of this destruction, a stream of manic laughter burst out of her.

"Just look at this," she shouted. "See what those demons have done to me!"

It seemed to me that she was really and truly happy about the destruction, as if it had come only to save her from her depression. Yet, no more than a few moments later, the laughter froze on her lips, her eyes glazed over, and a chill rage set her jaw. I knew this anger, and I was afraid of it. I waited for Maria to tell me what to do. It pained me that the hut, whose every corner was familiar to me, had been so totally wrecked. I saw the rafters scattered on the ground. For some reason, I started picking up the plates and the pots and pans that had fallen off the shelves, and I put them on the wooden counter that was used for preparing the meals. At first it seemed to me that Maria was happy that I was gathering the utensils, but a few seconds later she began shouting at me. "What are you doing, bastard? Who asked you to do this? Get out of here! Don't let me see your face," she screamed, and slapped me. But this time she didn't stop there, and with a stick in her hand she ran after me and knocked me down. I saw the stick and tried to get up, but I couldn't. In the end, just as a harnessed horse, whipped and whipped again, eventually drags itself out of the mire, I got to my feet and ran. I didn't go back to her.

More than fifty years have passed, and that fear is still within my legs. Sometimes it seems to me that the stick that she threw at me is still airborne. But, more than this humiliating parting from her, I remember how her face could suddenly change and radiate happiness. Her happiness, like her sadness, knew no bounds. When she was happy, she seemed to resemble the woman in the picture that hung at the head of her bed: young, crowned with wavy locks, wearing a summer dress that hung from two straps, tall and slender, and with a smile that lit up her face. That was apparently how she wished to see herself, or perhaps that is how she wanted to be remembered.

9

SOME SIGHTS ARE NOT easily forgotten. I was ten years old and I lived in the forest. Summer in the forest is full of surprises: a cherry tree here, and over there, growing close to the ground, a wild strawberry bush. It had been two weeks since it rained. My shoes and clothes had dried out, and I found the smell of mold seeping out of them rather pleasant. It seemed that if I could only find the right path, it would lead me straight to my parents.

The thought that my parents were waiting for me stayed with me, protecting me throughout the war. Paths did lead me out of the forest, but not to my parents. Every day I tried another path, and every day I was disappointed.

The vistas alongside the forest were open and full of light: field upon field of corn as far as the eye could see, out to the distant horizon. Sometimes I'd stand for hours and wait for my parents. Over time I made up omens in anticipation of their return: if the wind was strong . . . if I saw a white horse . . . if the sun set without a flaming sky. These omens brought inevitable disappointment, but for some reason I did not despair. I'd make up new omens, find new paths. For hours I'd sit by the banks of the stream and envision my parents returning to me.

Sometimes I'd be gripped by a deep sadness, a feeling that I'd die without ever seeing my parents again. I'd pictured my own death in various ways, sometimes as a kind of drifting up into the sky, higher and higher, and sometimes as being carried along upon the tops of the cornfields. It was clear to me that after my death I would no longer be lost. No longer would any omens mislead me, and there would be only one path that would lead me directly to my parents. On the route to the camp and during my time there I had seen many dying people, yet somehow I refused to see my own death as resembling theirs in any way.

On one of the very quiet days in the forest (most of the days were quiet, and apart from the shriek of birds of prey there were no discordant sounds), while I was standing at the edge of a cornfield, fascinated by its wavelike movement and by the green that changed from light to dark and then back again, I suddenly saw a small dark figure moving over the waves of corn. It seemed to me that he was swimming quite effortlessly. The small figure was far from me, and yet I could still see his movements very clearly.

As I was following this dark little figure, I heard muted voices from a distance, the sound of the wind mingling with the blustery voices of men. I looked around and saw nothing. The dark figure had advanced, and it seemed as though he was attempting to reach the forest. Straining to see from which direction the sounds were coming, I could make out a posse of men on the ridge next to me, which was also a cornfield. They were advancing as if on a raft. At first I didn't make the connection between the small figure that was swimming across the top of the cornfield and these other bodies that were also being borne aloft, but after a while I realized that their movements were accompanied by war cries, that they were fanning out to the sides and flanking him. The small figure, who at first had seemed to be swimming effortlessly, now appeared to be growing tired. The distance between him and the forest toward which he was aiming had not narrowed.

All this took place a few hundred meters from me, and although I saw the people, I connected these strong move-ments not with human beings but with nature. It seemed to me that the winds were gathering strength to leap forward and spread over the cornfields and cut them down.

It didn't take all that long for the truth to be revealed. The small figure was no more than a child, and those pursuing him, peasants. There were many peasants, with axes and scythes in their hands, pressing forward, determined to catch him. Now I saw the child's figure very clearly; he was breath-ing heavily and turning his head every few moments. It was clear that he wouldn't escape them. He couldn't escape. They were many and they could outrun him; soon they would be blocking his path.

I stood and looked at the swarthy, sturdy faces of the peasants and at the intensity of their advance. The child was trying very hard, but his efforts were in vain. Apparently he was caught not far from the forest; I heard him pleading with them.

After that, I saw the crowd of men return to the village. They were braying, exultant, as if after a successful hunt. Two young peasants dragged the child by his arms. I knew that soon, if he was still alive, they'd turn him over to the police, and in my heart I knew that my fate, when the time came, would be no different from his. Yet that night, when I laid my head down on the earth, I was happy to be alive and see the stars through the trees. This selfish feeling, which I knew to be impure, enfolded me, pulling me down into the depths of sleep.

10

I CAME ACROSS more than a few courageous and noble people during the war. Most memorable were the brothers Rauchwerger. Tall and sturdy, they looked like the Ruthenian peasants who worked in the warehouses. They had a non-Jewish type of naïveté that was evident in their every gesture. They trusted people and didn't bargain. Everyone cheated them, but they never got angry, never shouted or raised a hand.

Otto, the firstborn, had worked for many years in a lumberyard. The owner, a small shriveled Jew, exploited Otto's strength, working him late into the night. Otto neither complained nor demanded overtime pay. Occasionally he would go to the inn, down a few small glasses, and invite all the poor people there to join him for a drink. They loved him and would gather around him as if he were their elder brother. At the inn he'd be happy and throw his money around. Respectable people didn't like Otto. His naïveté and honesty were considered foolish. They'd say, "A man who doesn't stand up for what he thinks and doesn't insist on getting what he deserves is an idiot."

With the outbreak of war, all the warehouses were closed down and, like many others, Otto was left without work. He spent some days at the inn, frittered away what money he had, and when he no longer had a cent to his name, he went to the orphanage and worked there as a volunteer.

In the morning, he would chop wood and fill the water tanks, fetch groceries, and peel potatoes. In the evening, he would bathe the orphans as he sang to them and imitated animal sounds. Then he would sing them to sleep with lullabies. Those who knew him well said that his cheerfulness in the ghetto was astounding.

When the deportations began, Otto hid the orphans in basements, and from there he led them out through the sewers to peasant homes and monasteries. After all this activity, his face would be as radiant as that of a child.

The deportations, of course, did not pass him by. On the forced march across the Ukrainian steppes, he helped the weak and buried the dead. Over the course of the war, his face changed, his beard grew, and he came to look like a rabbi who had been reincarnated in a non-Jewish body.

I wasn't with him in the labor camp, but after the liberation I met up with him again. He was thin. A kind of spirituality radiated from his face. Most of the refugees looked wretched and were depressed, but Otto hadn't changed in the slightest: he had the same way of inclining his body toward you in careful attentiveness, the same natural desire to lend a hand and to help, the same self-effacement.

After the liberation, people hoarded food and clothing to a sickening extent. Otto didn't change his habits. What he had done in the ghetto, he did here, too. In the soup kitchen of the Joint Distribution Committee, he peeled potatoes and washed dishes.

During the war, people changed beyond recognition.

Decent people who had run large companies would steal bread under the cover of darkness, and overnight honest merchants turned into enemies of their own children. But there were also people, mainly simpler folk, who came into their own, totally devoting themselves to others. Such a one was the middle Rauchwerger brother, Max.

After Max's family had been rounded up and sent to the camps, leaving him all alone, he began to work as a volunteer in the hospital. He quickly gained a reputation for decency and devotion, and any time he appeared in the street to ask for donations for the sick, men and women would fill his basket with bread, salt, sugar, and candy for the children. People trusted him, freely giving him what they might have eaten themselves or kept for their own children. On more than one occasion, he was brought half an orange or half a lemon, "since it was more vital for the sick."

Only some months previously, Max had been selling coal under an awning he'd put up on an empty lot, waiting hours for buyers and eventually selling the coal for next to nothing. Not a trace remained of this person. Max's transformation was so complete that people didn't believe their own eyes. His bearing became more erect, and he stood head and shoulders above all others. Of his former occupation not a trace remained. He resembled one of the porters—sunburned, ready to put his shoulder to any load. There were people who said, "He's taken leave of his senses," but most knew that Max was completely devoted to the sick, fully immersed in his work—and not crazy.

He would labor from morning till late at night and sleep in a corner room next to the woodshed. When the sick were deported, Max went with them.

Karl, the youngest of the brothers, was a deaf-mute from birth. Because he was as tall and as sturdily built as his brothers, he earned his living as a porter, moving heavy things. He worked for the owner of a truck, a vulgar man who treated him abusively, kicking him and slapping his face. Karl, who was as innocent as a child, neither complained nor raised a hand to him, but worked from morning till night, barely making a living.

During the days of the ghetto, Karl returned to his former home: the Institution for Deaf-Mutes. The staff remembered him and welcomed him with open arms. The ghetto days became his hour of glory. Karl moved furniture, sacks of potatoes, barrels—anything and everything. He was greatly loved by the other deaf-mutes. If one of them was attacked, he would defend him with all his might.

Everyone wondered how these brothers had been raised, for they had not gone to high school and did not read newspapers. Their parents were simple folk, so what had they imbued their sons with to turn them into people with such a remarkable devotion to others? Nobody could come up with an answer.

The fate of young Karl was different from that of his two elder brothers. For no apparent reason, a Romanian officer attacked one of the deaf-mutes. Karl went up to the officer and asked him to leave the man alone. The officer began beating him, too. Karl stumbled and fell, but quickly picked himself up, caught the officer by his throat, and strangled him to death. Karl was immediately seized, and on that same night was taken out into the yard of the police station and shot.

11

IT WAS ONLY in Italy, after the war, that I heard about the Pen, a sort of animal enclosure that they called the Keffer. Refugees sat around in groups, talking loudly about the atrocities. Sometimes it seemed that they were competing among themselves—who had seen more and who had suffered more. We children didn't know how to tell our stories. We would sit and listen. Sometimes they would bother us with questions. During the years of the war, we had learned not to answer.

People told their stories and described what they had seen. But apparently not everything was discussed. There were atrocities that were beyond words, that remained dark secrets. This was the case, for example, with the Keffer. Whenever this name rose to someone's lips, the speaker would be silenced. One night I heard one of the refugees say, "There are atrocities that one should not speak about."

"Why?" wondered another refugee.

"I can't explain it to you."

"You have to speak about everything, so that everyone will know what they did to us."

"I'm not going to argue with you."

"If we won't be witnesses, who will bear witness?"

"They won't believe us, anyway."

As was the case with most arguments, this one settled nothing. Some atrocities were described in the most minute detail, and some atrocities no one dared talk about.

But one night I heard more about the Pen from a refugee who had come from the Kalschund camp. He was a short man, solid and broad-shouldered, and his sturdiness had in no way been diminished by the war. With a face as coarse as a boxer's, his very stance declared: I'm ready for another war.

He seemed not to be aware of the self-imposed taboo that the refugees placed on this subject. At first the others tried to stop him, but either he didn't get it or he pretended not to, and he stood up and spoke. "The Pen that was called Keffer was an integral part of the Kalschund camp, and from some angles I was able to see most of it. It was a pen for German shepherds that were used as guard dogs, for hunting, but mainly to chase after prisoners who had escaped. The dogs had been brought over from Germany already trained, and they were the pride of the guards and the officers. Toward evening, they would be let out to hunt, and then everyone could see how large and proud they were, and how much more they resembled wolves than dogs.

"The Kalschund camp was a labor camp for metal welding. It also produced ammunition. Only strong men were brought there, and, despite the extremely harsh conditions, they would usually last for a year or even longer. If women had somehow been mistakenly included in the transport, they would be beaten and returned. Once some elderly women were brought in on the transport, and they were immediately taken out to be killed. One day some small children were included in the transport. The camp commandant ordered them to be stripped and pushed into the Pen. The children must have been devoured instantly, for no screams were heard.

"This became routine. Any time small children arrived at the camp (and every month there were some), they would be stripped and pushed into the Pen.

"One day, something surprising happened: the dogs devoured whatever they devoured but two children were not harmed at all. And even more astonishing: the children just stood there stroking them. The dogs looked content, and the guards, too. From then on, the guards would throw pieces of meat to the dogs and pieces of bread and cheese to the children. The camp commandant would bring his guests to the Pen to show this to them. But eventually, even for these children, the Pen stopped being a safe place. German shepherds are German shepherds. When starved, they know no pity. Even these children, who were in the Pen for weeks, were devoured.

"Had it not been for the Pen, Kalschund would have been considered a bearable camp, but its existence made this labor camp into a death camp. At Kalschund people weren't taken out to be executed, but the sight of those children sent to their death utterly demoralized us. It was no wonder that we had so many suicides there."

The refugee continued, "Once we saw a child outside the Pen. He was crawling on all fours next to the barbed wire and gesturing to the dogs. What was outside apparently terrified him more than the dogs inside, and he returned to the Pen.

"One night, a child escaped from the Pen and somehow reached our barracks. He was a terrifying sight. His face and his neck had been mauled, but he didn't complain or cry. People tried in vain to get a word out of him. Eventually he uttered some syllables that were more like small growls.

"It was extremely dangerous, but we were prepared to

put our own lives at risk, and so we hid him inside a wooden crate. At night, we would take off the lid, give him water, and feed him. The knowledge that there was a child in the barracks changed our lives that autumn. There was fierce competition among us as to who would give the child his daily ration. All of us fought to give it to him.

"Sometimes it seemed that he was recovering and that his wounds were healing. Over time we improved upon the crate and made a place for a can of water. One night, when we removed the lid, we saw that the child wasn't breathing. We were too afraid to go out, so we buried him under the barracks. From then on, he was with us even more. For some reason, we were certain that one night he would get up and speak to us in his own voice.

"That's how it was until the Russians came. When the Russian army liberated the camp, there were two children in the Pen. They were taken out and brought to the room where interrogations were held. The children stared vacantly, stuttered in broken syllables, shrugged their shoulders—one of them even stamped his feet—but not a sentence escaped from them. The investigators tried to talk to them in a friendly way, first in Yiddish and then in Polish. At one point an elderly man was brought in who tried to talk to them in Hungarian, but it was no use. Though the children had survived, language had been completely torn from their throats.

"Then one of the survivors burst in; stuttering, and with great emotion, he told the investigators about the Pen and about what had been done to children there. The investigators didn't believe him and asked that another witness be brought. The next witness, a tall and lean man, confirmed it: since he worked next to the furnaces and had an unimpeded view of the Pen, he had seen with his own eyes how the dogs had devoured the children."

The refugee lowered his voice and continued: "At Kalschund the survivors didn't disperse immediately after the liberation. A medic bathed the two children and bandaged their wounds. There was a terrifying vacancy in their eyes. Most of the day they sat on their beds, frozen in silence. But eventually, like the adult survivors, they started to fight and had to be separated."

12

TERRIBLE PEOPLE—corrupt and violent—preyed upon us all the way from the Ukraine to Italy. Most abhorrent of all were the perverts. They would seduce children and do painful things to them before letting them go. The children who were abused neither complained nor cried. A kind of silent expression settled onto their faces, as if a secret was sealed up inside them. They carried this secret for many years, through their time in the youth village, and sometimes even into their military service.

During my first year at university, I saw a young man of around my age whose lips were pursed like those of the children who had been abused. I made no overtures to him. To my surprise, he addressed me, asking for my notes, since he had missed three lectures. I wasn't wrong: he had been in the ghetto and in a concentration camp and, like me, survived only by miracle. After the liberation, he had indeed made that tortuous journey from the Ukraine to Italy. He arrived in Palestine two months after I did.

Two days later, he returned my notebook and thanked me, but we didn't arrange to meet. Afterward I noticed that he avoided me, as if he sensed that I knew something of his secret. So that he wouldn't feel threatened, I also distanced myself from him.

Although we were surrounded by evil people after the war, there were also some who increased in stature as a result of it. Their walk slowed, their expressions became more open, and their faces glowed with a kind of spirituality. They were for the most part educated people, but simple folk also attained these heights.

Unlike the rest of the refugees, these people didn't hoard food or deal on the black market. Most of the time they kept to themselves; people like these were to be found in every convoy and in every displaced-persons camp. When the DP camps grew larger, they would sometimes become the youth leaders and the teachers, and they defended the children with all their might. They struggled not only against the smugglers, the middlemen, those illegally crossing borders, and the perverts, but also against people from the Joint Distribution Committee who didn't want to allocate space for classrooms, and who skimped on writing pads and books. ·

Amid the greed, bribery, and corruption, these exceptional people not only taught the children to read and write, but also taught us mathematics, Hebrew, Yiddish, and French, and they read to us from the Bible. There were also musicians, who taught us music. We children had the privilege of finding ourselves, albeit for a short time, in the company of wonderful people. Among them were high-school teachers and university lecturers whom the war had stripped of their degrees, their social standing, and their careers. Now all they asked was to help those who had suffered the most. But it wasn't always in their power to protect the children. The DP camps were completely exposed. All kinds of smugglers and perverted characters lay in ambush in every corner. And, it must be said, not all the children wanted to learn. There were children who, after a couple of days of study, would run back to the smugglers. The teachers would pursue them in the hope of saving them, but the smugglers were quicker.

There were exceptional children among the survivors, children who had flawless memories or highly developed musical talent, and there were even ten- or eleven-year-olds who spoke several languages fluently.

It turned out that the forests and the hiding places had not only distorted young lives, but had also nurtured unusual talent. For these children, it was not the smugglers who lay in ambush but the handlers. They would kidnap children, blindfold them, put them in trucks, and transport them to distant places. All along the coast of Italy were DP camps filled with scores of people, and everyone was in search of entertainment.

The poet Y.S., a short, unimpressive man, bald and thin, was our teacher. From up close he looked like one of the dealers. But the moment he opened his mouth, you were captivated by his voice. He taught us poetry and singing—all in Yiddish. He would pit himself against the youth leaders who had been sent from Palestine. They advocated Hebrew; he, Yiddish. They were taller than he was and better-looking and, most important, they spoke in the name of the future, in the name of change that was all to the good, and they spoke about the life that awaited us in Palestine. He, naturally, spoke about what had been, about continuity, and how there could be no continuity if we didn't know the language of the persecuted. He used to say that whoever speaks the language of those tortured people not only keeps their memory alive in this world, but also staves off evil.

During that time, the DP camps were like battlefields.

Sometimes it seemed that all the struggles were over the children and who would claim them. Would the smugglers succeed in fanning them out over the continent, or would the soldiers of the Jewish Brigade protect them and bring them to Palestine? Or perhaps some distant relatives would lure them to America?

The poet Y.S. was the most courageous of the defenders. Any time he saw a smuggler or handler attempting to enslave a child, he would stand up and cry out, "The God of Justice will not forgive you!" They of course would heap scorn and ridicule upon him, calling him all kinds of names, and on more than one occasion they beat him up. These beatings in no way deterred him; he would denounce them, get up, and never miss a class.

Y.S. taught us for three months. He started out with seventeen children, but over time the smugglers and the handlers tempted away six, so only eleven remained. At night we would sleep with the windows closed, and Y.S. would block the door with his bed. He didn't only teach us poetry. For hours he would talk to us about the Ba'al Shem Tov, about his great-grandson, Rabbi Nachman of Bratslav, and about the small towns to which the teachers of Hasidism would journey as they taught love of one's fellow man and love of God. Y.S. did not wear a *kippah,* nor did he pray, but he was extremely devoted to the teachers of Hasidism and would call them "holy people of God."

At the end of the summer, the handlers tried to kidnap Miliu, a child from our group who had a remarkable singing voice. Twice they broke into the hut and tried to snatch him. Y.S. fought back with all his strength and saved him. But the handlers were undeterred. One night, three of them broke in and kidnapped Miliu. Y.S. was very badly hurt trying to protect him. The next day, he was taken to a hospital in Naples.

After that it began to rain heavily. The Italian police sealed off the camp and conducted searches. The traders and smugglers tried in vain to protect their goods. Suitcases were confiscated and loaded onto two trucks. After the trucks left the camp with the contraband, people pounced upon a man named Shmil and accused him of informing. He denied it, claiming that he was a good Jew and that one Jew doesn't snitch on another. The traders and smugglers didn't believe him; they were sure he had squealed on them, and started to beat him. He screamed and begged, but the more he begged, the more they beat him. Eventually he fell silent, and died all curled up.

After the murder, we left the camp with our teacher, Y.S., and moved with him into an abandoned hut by the beach.

13

IT WAS NOT from a pleasant man that I learned to pray. At the time, I was in a transit camp on my way to Palestine, in one of the long and shabby barracks into which hundreds of survivors were crammed. Men played cards, drank vodka, and had sex with women in broad daylight. In the dark corners of those same barracks, people stood and prayed in the morning and in the evening. Not many. It was always difficult to gather together ten men for a *minyan*. After the war, the lust for life was strong, and praying was derided; people refused to join in, even as bystanders. First persuasion, and then pleading was necessary.

It would have been easier had it been possible to pray alone. But what can one do? Jews are commanded to pray together.

At the entrance to each barrack, a short, drab man, quite undistinguished, would stand, morning and evening, exhorting men to join the prayers. However, since this lobbying didn't work, others would add to it the threat of divine punishment, awakening old feelings of guilt. It was no wonder that such people were scorned. They were abused, called all kinds of names, and, when they continued to threaten God's wrath, beaten without mercy.

And yet, somehow, a *minyan* would always be formed in the morning and in the evening. Men did come, either willingly or through coercion. This perseverance drove people crazy. Not a day went by without arguments, mutual recriminations, and curses. And, as is the case with every battle, words that hadn't been heard for years were dredged up from oblivion. I was then thirteen years old and keenly felt the need to pray. Those praying did not take kindly to my presence, looking askance—even scornfully—at me, but I, for some reason, did not skip even one *minyan*. The melody—the mournful, monotonic melody—enchanted me.

"Perhaps you could teach me to pray?" I asked one of the men.

"Whatever for?" he said, without even glancing in my direction.

Another person who heard my request added, "It's no simple matter—it's a whole business. Why would you need it?"

At that time, again, children were in danger. Handlers, moneychangers, smugglers, and ordinary thieves made them carry out dangerous missions. On more than one occasion, a child fell into the hands of the police and often was beaten because he was afraid to inform on those who had dispatched him. There were also the daredevil children who worked in gangs, moving goods from place to place and spending their nights in the whorehouses of Naples. No one dared to raise a finger against them. Anyone who harmed them put himself in danger, for they were absolutely fearless. Three gangs of children roamed around Naples at that time. Sometimes war would break out among them. These were real battles that left people injured and dead, but most children were weak and passive and did what the grown-ups told them to do.

I once again summoned up my courage and asked one of those praying to teach me. He looked at me sharply and asked, "Why didn't you learn at home?"

"My parents weren't religious," I said truthfully.

"If they weren't religious, why should you be religious?"

I didn't know what to answer, so I simply said, "I want to pray."

"You don't know what you want," he said, and turned his back on me.

As fall approached, the barracks began to empty. Some of the survivors sailed off to Palestine; most went to Australia and America. It was cold outside. The poker games heated up, and some fights broke out. One of the smugglers tried to get me to join his gang, to earn fifty dollars on one run. I had heard a lot about these sorties, about the clashes with the border police, and about informers who turned in the smugglers. They would mostly go out in groups of seven, of whom one was always caught or killed.

The desire to pray grew stronger within me from day to day. It became an unslakable, unaccountable thirst, one that would return anew every day to torment me. One of the men in the *minyan* noticed my distress and spoke to me quietly. "You'll be sailing to Palestine soon," he said. "In Palestine they work on kibbutzim and they don't pray."

Finally, one of the dealers agreed to teach me. He was a sturdy fellow with an unpleasant appearance who would hum and gabble his words. He read the large letters at the beginning of the faded prayer book to me a few times, and then said offhandedly, "Now go practice."

I practiced for two days. Apparently without success. Whenever I made a mistake, he would slap my face. I could have left the place and gone to another camp, but for some reason I was convinced that learning to pray was bound up with suffering, so I accepted it. One of the worshippers saw the slaps I was being dealt and turned to my teacher. "Why are you hitting the orphan?" he asked.

"To get the letters into his head."

"Orphans shouldn't be hit."

"Ach, it won't hurt him."

Learning the Hebrew alphabet was hard for me, and I was often close to leaving both the place and the man, but for some reason I didn't. Another one of the refugees who saw my distress couldn't restrain himself. "Boys your age are already doing more important things," he said. "Haven't you learned your lesson?"

I didn't know which lesson he meant. At any rate, I loved to pray. The thought that one day I, too, would be able to stand, prayer book in hand, and pray, was stronger than the humiliation. That strong man had no pity on me. Sometimes it seemed to me that he was hitting me in order to uproot my desire to pray.

For two months I studied prayers with this man, whose name was Pini. Then he obtained a visa and sailed off to Australia. He parted from the *minyan* with a bottle of liquor. His friends in the black market didn't seem particularly happy for him. Me, he avoided.

I was glad that he had sailed off. His indifference and his cold anger continued to scare me long after he had gone, although the prayers that he had left me with gave me great pleasure.

A month after he departed, prayer started to flow out of my mouth. The feeling that I was able to follow the man who led the prayers, to repeat his verses along with everyone else, infused me with courage. Even the drab dealers, indifferent and selfish, seemed friendly to me.

I was mistaken, of course. One of those who came to pray suggested that I smuggle cigarettes to Sicily. When I refused, he said threateningly, "You watch out! If I catch you here, you'll regret it."

The threat sounded real to me, and I stopped coming to *minyan*. Fortunately for me, later that same week we moved to another camp, and my desire to pray was sent into hiding.

14

THE WAR SPAWNED many strange children, but Chico
was one of a kind. His memory, it was said, was phenomenal.
He could repeat thirty numbers as if they were but three, and
he would do so without making a single error. The first time I
saw him was in the refugee camp in Italy, on the way to Palestine. He was part of a troupe of child performers between the
ages of seven and eight. Among them were jugglers and fire-
eaters, and a child who walked a tightrope that he had strung
between the trees. There was also a girl singer, Amalia, who
had the voice of a nightingale. She did not sing in any particular language, but in one all her own, a mixture of words
that she remembered from home, sounds from the pastures,
noises from the forest, and prayers from the convent. People
would listen to her and weep. It was hard to tell exactly what
she sang about. It always seemed as though she was telling a
long story full of hidden details. Her seven-year-old friend
would dance alongside her, or sometimes he would dance
alone. Amalia loved watching him and, though she was his

age, or perhaps even younger, she would gaze at him like an older sister. Her look was mature and full of concern, as if she wanted to shield him under her wing. There was also a child who played sad Russian songs on his harmonica. He was six years old, but looked younger. They made a crate for him, and he'd stand on it and play.

These little troupes sprang up on the roads and wandered from camp to camp, and at night they would entertain those who were tired of the war and of themselves. At that time people didn't know what to do with themselves, with lives that had been so unexpectedly spared. There were no words; the ones left over from home sounded hollow. Sometimes a man would appear and words would flow from his mouth. But the words he used were from before the war, and they sounded like coarse scraps, devoid of all taste. Only the speech of the small children still had some kind of freshness. I say small children, because the twelve- and thirteen-year-olds were already corrupt: they traded, changed money, pilfered, and robbed like the grown-ups. But, unlike the grown-ups, they were agile. The years in the forests had taught them how to move quickly, how to climb and to scurry about. They had learned much from the animals they had observed there.

We did not yet realize that the children had created a new language. Their language emerged from their very being, from the way they stood or sat, sang or spoke. It was straightforward, and it hid nothing.

CHICO WAS THEN seven years old, and his memory astounded his audience. His handler eventually taught him to tell stories, and he would perform them without slipping up at all. But the streetwise handler quickly understood that Chico was a gold mine, and he acted accordingly. He taught Chico some of the psalms and the Kaddish. He taught him to pray in the old-fashioned way, for the handler was himself a cantor's son.

Within a short time, Chico knew the verses by heart, and he soon overshadowed all the other children in the troupe. He always appeared at the end and stole the show. Chico's prayer was admittedly different from anything that had ever been heard before. Neither a lamentation nor a supplication, it was an utterly simple devotion known only to our forefathers.

All eyes were fixed on Chico. He gave them what they needed at that moment: a little of that sense of belief that they had almost forgotten, a connection to the dear ones they had lost. It was hard to know if Chico understood what was coming out of his mouth. In any case, his prayer was so lucid and artless and pure that people hearing it wept like children.

Because Chico was such a success, his fellows in the troupe stopped appearing, and Chico's act filled the entire evening. "He's just a baby," people said. "He's a *Wunderkind*, a prodigy, a reincarnation. In your entire life, have you ever seen a child of seven who knew the entire prayer book by heart?!"

His handler raked in the cash and hustled his little troupe from place to place. Chico appeared evening after evening, and sometimes during the day as well. The handler took care to provide him with food and drink, and if Chico refused to eat, he would reprimand and force him. Chico ate and grew fat. But, wonder of wonders, despite growing fat and despite having to give so many performances, Chico didn't lose the purity of his prayer.

From week to week, his voice became purer. Anyone who heard Chico once would be drawn to him again. And so it went on for the entire summer. In the winter the handler fixed up an abandoned hut, filled it with benches, and posted a guard at the entrance. He was sure that now his earnings would only increase.

But the hut, which had held out great promise, didn't bring luck. On the opening night Chico caught a cold, took to his bed, and burned with fever. His fever raged on for two weeks, and when he finally rose from his sickbed, the prayers had been erased from his memory. In vain did the handler try to teach them to him all over again. A blue, bewildered sort of gaze now settled in Chico's eyes, as if he didn't understand what people were saying to him.

"Chico! Chico!" The handler would shake him. But Chico was never the same again.

Out of sheer desperation, the handler put Amalia and her partner back onstage, with the child who played the harmonica. They were excellent, surpassing themselves, but they were unable to compete with Chico. "Where's Chico?" rumbled the audience. The handler had no choice but to put him onstage, so that everyone could see that he was still alive. But Chico, who only a month ago had climbed nimbly onto the stage and launched straight into a prayer, stood there frozen. His blue eyes were filled with a frighteningly vacant expression.

And thus was Chico's star extinguished. Amalia and her partner and the other members of the troupe made tremendous efforts, but people were not prepared to pay a lot of money for their performances. At night the handler would blast Chico for his laziness and for not even trying to make an effort. Finally, he threatened to send him to Palestine, where it was tremendously hot and people worked from morning till night. It was hard to know what Chico was thinking. The handler's words apparently hurt him, because his mouth puckered up and his right shoulder jerked uncontrollably. Though

the troupe suffered at the hands of their impresario, the children did not leave him. "Run away!" people would urge them,
but they seemed to be used to him and his excesses.

At the end of the winter, some people set upon the handler and beat him up. He didn't give in easily. He whined and
shouted, "The children are mine, and mine alone. I'm their
mentor, and I've looked after them since the end of the war."

But his entreaties were useless. While he was lying on
the ground, bleeding profusely, the children were hoisted up
onto a truck and taken straight to the shore, where a ship was
anchored.

Throughout the entire trip from Naples to Haifa, evening after evening and sometimes during the day as well, the
troupe would perform on the deck. Although Chico's memory
never returned, he would recite the prayer "God Full of Mer-
cies" with great feeling. His face matured, so that he looked
older than he actually was—more like a nine-year-old. A
large woman from Transylvania wrapped him in a sweater and
did not move from his side during the entire voyage.

15

WORLD WAR II WENT ON for six straight years, but sometimes it seems to me that it lasted only one long night, from which I awoke a completely different person. Sometimes I felt that it wasn't I who was in the war, but someone else, someone very close to me, and that he was going to tell me what exactly occurred, for I don't remember what happened or how it happened.

I say "I don't remember," and that's the whole truth. The strongest imprints those years have left on me are intense physical ones. The hunger for bread. To this very day I can wake up in the middle of the night ravenously hungry. Dreams of hunger and thirst haunt me almost on a weekly basis. I eat as only people who have known hunger eat, with a strangely ravenous appetite.

During the course of the war, I was in hundreds of places—in railway stations, in remote villages, on the banks of rivers. All these places had names, but there's not one that I can remember. Sometimes I see the war years like a large pasture that blends into the horizon; sometimes it's like a dark and gloomy forest that goes on interminably; and sometimes it's like a long line of people weighed down with bundles and knapsacks. From time to time some of the people collapse onto the ground, only to be trampled by all the other feet.

Everything that happened is imprinted within my body and not within my memory. The cells of my body apparently remember more than my mind, which is supposed to remember. For years after the war, I would walk neither in the middle of the sidewalk nor in the middle of the road. I always clung to the walls, always staying in the shade, and always walking rapidly, as if I were slipping away. As a rule I'm not given to crying, but even the most casual partings can reduce me to tears.

I say "I don't remember," and yet I still recall thousands of details. Sometimes just the aroma of a certain dish or the dampness of shoes or a sudden noise is enough to take me back into the middle of the war, and then it seems to me that it never really ended, but that it has continued without my knowledge. And now that I am fully aware of it, I realize that there's been no letup since it began.

Because I spent a large part of the war in villages, in fields, by riverbanks, and in forests, this greenness is imprinted on me, and whenever I remove my shoes and step on the grass, I immediately remember the pastures and the dappled animals scattered over the endless space. And then a fear of these open spaces returns to me. My legs feel tense, and for a moment it seems to me that I've made a mistake. I'm still in the war, and I have to beat a retreat to the outer edges of the forest, running and ducking, because the outer edges provide more safety. At the edges of the forest you can see without being seen. Sometimes I find myself in a dark alley—as one can in Jerusalem—and I'm sure that the gate will soon be closed and I won't be able to get out. I quicken my pace and try to get away.

Sometimes the very act of sitting down or standing up brings to mind visions of a railway station filled with people and baggage, with arguments and children being slapped, with arms and hands thrust out in continuous entreaty. "Water, water!" And suddenly hundreds of legs raise themselves, moving as one toward a water barrel that is being rolled onto the platform, and the sole of a large foot pushes into my frail chest, crushing the breath out of me. It's unbelievable, how the sole of that same foot is still imprinted on me, how fresh the pain is, and for a moment it seems to me that I can't move because of it.

Sometimes a month goes by without anything of what I saw during that time coming back to me. Of course, this is merely a temporary hiatus. Sometimes just an old object, lying on the roadside, is enough to draw up hundreds of feet from the depths, feet that are marching in a long column. And if anyone collapses under it, no one will help him get up.

IN 1944, the Russians recaptured the Ukraine. I was twelve years old. A woman survivor who noticed me and saw how lost I was, bent down and asked, "What have you been through, boy?"

"Nothing," I replied.

My answer must have astonished her, for she didn't ask me anything else. This same question was asked in different ways on my long journey to Yugoslavia. Even in Israel there was no end to it.

Someone who was an adult during the war took in and remembered places and individuals, and at the end of the war he could sit and recall them, or talk about them. (As he would no doubt continue to do till the end of his life.) With us children, however, it was not names that were sunk into memory, but something completely different. For a child, memory is a reservoir that doesn't empty. It's replenished over the years, clarified. It's not a chronological recollection, but overflowing and changing, if I may put it that way.

I've already written more than twenty books about those years, but sometimes it seems as though I haven't yet begun to describe them. Sometimes it seems to me that a fully detailed memory is still concealed within me, and when it emerges from its bunker, it will flow fiercely and strongly for days on end. This is a fragment about a forced march that I've been trying to describe, without success, for years.

WE'VE ALREADY BEEN MARCHING for days, slogging through muddy roads, a long line surrounded by Romanian soldiers and Ukrainian militia who lash out at us with their whips and shoot randomly at us. Father holds my hand very tightly. But my short legs barely touch the ground, and the icy water cuts into them and into my small waist. Darkness surrounds us, and apart from Father's hand, I don't feel a thing. In fact, I don't even feel his hand, for my arm is already partially numb. It's clear to me that with only one small wrong movement I'll sink down and I'll drown, and even Father won't be able to pull me out. Many children have already drowned like this.

At night, when the convoy stops, Father pulls me out of the mud and wipes my legs with his coat. My shoes were lost some time ago, and I bury my legs for a moment in the lining of his coat. The slight warmth hurts me so much that I quickly pull them out. For some reason, this rapid movement makes him angry. Father can get bitterly angry at me. I'm afraid of his anger, but I refuse to put my legs into his lining. Father never used to get angry at me. Mother would slap me from time to time, but never Father. If Father is angry, that means that I'm going to die soon, I tell myself, and grip his hand tightly. Father relents and says, "This is no time to act spoiled." "Spoiled"—a word that Mother would frequently use—now sounds strange. As if Father is wrong, or perhaps I am. Without letting go of his hand I drop off to sleep, but not for long.

While the sky is still dark, the soldiers wake up the convoy with whippings and shootings. Father grabs my hand and pulls me up. The mud is deep, and I cannot feel any solid ground beneath it. I'm still drowsy from sleep, and my fear is dulled. "It hurts me!" I call out. Father hears my cry and responds instantly, "Make it easier for me, make it easier."

I've heard those words often. After them come a dreadful collapse and the futile attempts to save a child who has drowned. Not only children drown in the mud; even tall people sink into it, fall to their knees, and drown. Spring is melting the snows, and with every passing day the mud gets deeper. Father opens his knapsack and tosses some of the clothes into the mud. Now his hand holds mine with great strength. At night he rubs my arms and legs and wipes them with the lining of his coat, and for a moment it seems to me that not only my father is with me, but also my mother, whom I loved so much.

16

I MET MANY devoted people on the long route from the Ukrainian steppes to the Haifa coast. On the ship, or, more precisely, on the ship's deck, where people and their belongings were all jumbled up together, I saw a man, no longer young, holding in his arms a little girl who was around five years old. She was a joyful child, and her shining face made everyone around her happy. Dressed in a nice wool dress, she didn't seem like a survivor. She spoke Jewish German and sang in a pleasant voice. While everyone else became seasick or ill from the food, or stiff with weariness, her every movement was filled with grace. It turned out that the man taking care of her was not her father, but he was even more devoted than a father. He hung on her every word, gazing at her with astonishment.

The ship made its way through a stormy sea, its deck filled with hundreds of people: vulgar men and large, irritable women. Most of them became sick, moaning and vomiting, but little Helga alone did not complain. In fact, the greater

the commotion on the deck, the brighter her face became—
not that anyone really paid attention to her. Everyone was
absorbed in his own suffering. It brought to mind the train
stations where, not so very long ago, people had been packed
onto the cattle cars.

No sooner had the storm subsided than the sun came
out. The sea calmed, and people emerged from the heap of
bags and packages and stood by the railing. It was then that
we saw that Helga's right leg had been amputated above her
knee. The amputation had apparently been done not too long
ago. The stump was still bandaged.

The man who had adopted her removed the bandages
and put on fresh ones. "Does it hurt?" he asked.

"No," Helga answered, smiling, as if he were talking
about some minor injury. Then she got up onto his lap. People
gathered around them, staring. In a monotone, the man told
how, some months earlier, he had found Helga lying on a pile
of straw. She had smiled and stretched out her hand to him.
"What could I do?" he said, smiling. "An angel, truly an
angel. You can't refuse angels, can you?"

"And why did they amputate her leg?"

"Because of the infection. The army doctors said that it
was endangering not only the rest of her leg, but her life as
well."

"And what do you have to do now?" They kept asking
him questions.

"Nothing in particular. The stump is healing. It looks a
lot better now."

"And will the girl be able to walk?"

"I have no doubt about it," said the man. "In Palestine
we'll have an artificial leg made for her. Helga very much
wants to walk."

"Who were her parents?"

"That's a riddle to be solved in the years to come," he said dryly, in a voice that seemed out of place.

"And you have no clues?"

"I have, but they're very slight ones."

"Helga, my dear, don't you remember anything?" A tall woman knelt down before her, astonishing everyone.

Helga smiled. "I remember the rain," she said.

"What rain are you talking about, my dear?" the woman asked in a soft voice.

"The rain that fell without stopping."

"And what happened then?" the large woman persisted.

"I got wet," she said, more in wonderment than as a statement of fact.

"And weren't you cold?" The woman continued to interrogate her in a soft voice.

"No," said Helga.

"And who was with you?"

"The rain, only the rain."

"And no one was at your side?"

"Perhaps there was, but I didn't see."

"Strange," said the large woman.

Helga licked her lips and didn't respond.

"And how long did the rain last?"

"All the time," said Helga, lifting her head.

"Strange," the large woman repeated.

People stood around in silence, as if they realized they were witnessing an extraordinary conversation.

"And what happened after the rain?"

"I don't remember," said Helga in a clear voice.

"And the rain continued falling all the time?" the woman mused.

"The pits filled up with water."

"And you, what did you do?"

"Nothing," said Helga, as if at last able to find the right word.

"She's a very wise child," the man who had adopted her intervened.

The large woman stood up but would not stop questioning Helga.

Then, for some reason, people expected the girl to tell her story. Helga hung her head and uttered not a sound. The light in her face seemed to fade.

"And you don't miss the rain?" the large woman repeated.

"No," said Helga in a clear voice.

"You shouldn't be asking her," an elderly man interrupted.

"Why?" wondered the large woman.

"Because you mustn't confuse her."

"I'm only asking," said the large woman, blushing.

"Your questions are confusing. Leave her alone."

"We love her," said the large woman.

"Why are you speaking for everyone?" the old man asked aggressively.

"That's what I feel."

"Let everyone speak for himself."

The last sentence left people feeling confused and dejected. They dispersed as if they had been reprimanded.

Helga sat on the lap of the man who had adopted her. The light returned to her face. She moved her lips, muttering softly. The man took her small hand, brought it to his lips, and kissed it. "Soon we'll reach Palestine," he said. "There we'll have a house and a garden."

17

FROM MY EARLIEST CHILDHOOD, I've had a tendency to approach both people and objects carefully, and with suspicion. Mother attributed this to the severe illnesses of my infancy; Grandmother claimed that only children are suspicious by nature. And, indeed, I was an only child, extremely attached to my parents. The area outside my house, particularly when I was there alone, seemed cold and threatening. Most of my childhood dreams (it's strange to what extent I can recall them) are linked to a sense of abandonment. I hold out my hand and the hand remains suspended in the air. I am immediately gripped with fear. I would wake up in the middle of the night trembling all over, and Mother would hasten to reassure me that it was just "a mistake of a dream," that she would never abandon me, that we would always be together. For some reason these promises only intensified my insecurities, and I would sob inconsolably until completely exhausted.

My feelings of distrust intensified when I started going to school. I was one of two Jewish children in a class of forty. I was puny, and well dressed, and Mother would walk me all the way to the school gate. This only increased the ridicule. During recess, everyone would be out in the yard, playing with a red rubber ball, kicking up dust and screaming. I would stand at the window and look out. Even then I knew: I would never be able to play like them. This was painful, but it was also amusing: a blend of feelings of inferiority and superiority. I was able to entertain myself with these feelings as long as I stayed out of the range of their hands; too near them, and I was an easy target for kicking, slapping, or pinching.

The non-Jewish children were taller and sturdier than I was, and I knew that even if I made a huge effort I wouldn't be able to close the gap. They would always rule the long corridors and the schoolyard. Their whim dictated whether I would be beaten or left alone. Common sense told me to get used to it, but a feeling of outrage occasionally got the better of me. Sometimes I would stand on the stairs and scream at the top of my voice, more than anything to overcome the fear that gripped me.

Mother tried to intervene by seeing the headmaster, but it was useless. There were thirty-eight sturdy bodies against me, a tide of legs that swept away anything that happened to be in its path—myself included.

I did try to defend myself a few times. It made not the slightest impression on the gang. On the contrary, it gave them an excuse to beat me up even more, and to claim that I had started it. The other Jewish boy deserted me in this futile struggle. Within a short time he changed beyond recognition, and although he was thinner than I was, he fitted well into the playground games. His agility more than made up for his lack of strength. He eventually turned his back on me, as though he and I were no longer members of the same tribe.

Every single day, from early in the morning (in winter,

from the dark hours of the dawn) until three in the afternoon, I was trapped with this wild herd. It's no wonder that I can't remember even one name, not even the name of the Jewish teacher, who herself had to contend with this mob, which already, at the age of seven, was charged with destructive energy. Like me, she stood helpless, shouting in vain, provoking waves of laughter. I don't recall faces, but I clearly remember the wide stone staircase, the gloomy, damp corridors, the tide of legs that would sweep over everything and hurtle out. I remember the school janitors who supervised the schoolyard. Cold and cunning, they were the supreme arbiters and would instill fear in everyone. If a child got out of control, they would tie him up and give him ten lashes. After receiving his punishment, the child had to kiss the hand of the one who had lashed him, say, "As you command, Father," and then leave the area. This ritual was repeated several times a week.

Mother was often on the verge of withdrawing me from this school, but Father wouldn't let her. He claimed that such was life, and that I'd better toughen up to it. Mother feared that I was suffering too much, but Father stood firm, as if he guessed that experiences harsher than this awaited me.

At the end of my first school year, my formal education came to an end. World War II broke out, turning everything upside down. Within a few weeks, the seven-year-old who had been enveloped in so much love and warmth had lost his mother and became an abandoned ghetto child, and eventually this child wound up trudging alongside his father on a forced march across the Ukrainian steppes. The dying lay beside the dead along the road, and the child limped on with his remaining strength, accompanied by the few who could still walk.

These sights remain within me as very clear memories. Sometimes it seems to me that the march, which lasted for about two months, has continued for the last fifty years, and that I'm still limping along on it.

After two months of walking we arrived—very few of us, indeed—at that accursed camp. Not many days passed before I was separated from my father and I escaped from the camp. From that moment, I was an orphan, and now began the loneliness and the closing off. Quickly I learned to speak little and, if questioned, to reply as briefly as possible.

During the war, I honed my sense of suspicion into a fine art. Before approaching a house, a stable, or a barn, I would bend down to the ground and listen, sometimes for hours. By the sounds, I could tell if there were people there, and how many. People were always a sign of danger. I spent much of the war flat on the ground, listening. Among other things, I learned to listen to the birds. They are remarkable harbingers, not only of imminent rain, but also of bad people and wild beasts.

From my days of wandering in the fields and in the forests, I learned to prefer the forest to the open fields, stables to houses, the deformed to those who were healthy, village outcasts to supposedly respectable homeowners. Sometimes reality would catch me unaware, but, for the most part, my suspicions proved themselves. Over time I learned that objects and animals are true friends. In the forest I was surrounded by trees, bushes, birds, and small animals. I was not afraid of them. I was sure that they would do nothing harmful to me. I became familiar with cows and with horses, and they provided me with a warmth that has remained with me to this very day. Sometimes it seemed to me that what saved me were the animals I encountered along the way, not the human beings. The hours I spent with puppies, cats, and sheep were the best of the war years. I would blend in with them until I was part of them, until forgetfulness came, until I fell asleep alongside them. I would sleep as deeply and as tranquilly as I had in my parents' bed.

I've noticed that those of my generation, particularly those who were children at the time of the war, developed suspicious attitudes toward people. People are unpredictable. A man who at first glance may appear calm or rational might turn out to be a savage person, or even a murderer.

After I left Maria, the woman who had taken me in, I worked for a blind old peasant. At first I was glad that he was blind, but it quickly became clear that he was no less cruel than the sighted peasants. Whenever he suspected that I wasn't doing my work as I should, or that I had been surreptitiously eating when I was supposed to be working, he would call me over to him and slap my face. In fact, whenever I was near him he would lunge forward and hit me with his sinewy hand. Once, when he seemed to think that I had drunk from the bucket of milk into which I had done the milking, he pushed me down to the ground and stomped on me. Yet I noticed that he would approach the animals in the barn quietly and gently, stroking their heads and whispering endearments to them. It was on me that he vented his anger, which was venomous, as if he blamed me for everything bad that had gone wrong with his life.

For about two years I lived out in the fields and surrounded by forests. There are sights that have been etched into my memory, and there is much that I have forgotten, but distrust has remained engraved on my body; even today, I stop and listen every few paces. Speech does not come easily to me, and it's no wonder: we didn't speak during the war. It was as though every disaster defied utterance: there was nothing to say. Anyone who was in the ghetto, in the camp, or hiding in the forests knows silence in his body. In time of war you don't argue, you don't sharpen differences of opinion. War is a hothouse for listening and for keeping silent. The hunger for bread, the thirst for water, the fear of death—all these make words superfluous. There's really no need for them. In the ghetto and in the camp, only people who had lost their minds talked, explained, or tried to persuade. Those who were sane didn't speak.

I've carried with me my mistrust of words from those years. A fluent stream of words awakens suspicion within me. I prefer stuttering, for in stuttering I hear the friction and the disquiet, the effort to purge impurities from the words, the desire to offer something from inside you. Smooth, fluent sentences leave me with a feeling of uncleanness, of order that hides emptiness.

That old axiom that a man is judged by his deeds seemed all the more true during the war. In the ghetto and in the camps, I saw many educated people, including renowned doctors and lawyers, who were prepared to kill for a piece of bread. But at the same time I saw people who knew how to relinquish, to give, to be totally self-effacing, and then to die without harming anyone or making anyone feel guilty. The war revealed more than superficial character traits; it also laid bare people's basic nature, whose foundation, as it turns out, is not only darkness. The selfish and the evil left me with a residue of fear and disgust; the generous bequeathed to me the warmth of their generosity. When I remember them, I'm overcome with shame for not possessing a fraction of their goodness.

During the war, we got to see the value of different ideologies. Some communists who preached equality and the love of one's fellow man in the town squares turned into beasts when truly tested. But there were also communists for whom the belief in their fellow man became so purified that up close they seemed like religious people. Everything they did was with the utter devotion of body and soul. It seemed to me that this rule applied to religious people as well. There were those who followed Jewish traditions but whom the war made heartless and selfish; and there were those who elevated God's commandments to ever higher degrees of light.

During the war, words had less currency than faces and hands. From the faces you learned to what extent the person next to you wanted to help you or intended to harm you. Words did not help one understand. The senses were what provided you with correct information. Starvation reverts us to our instincts, to a kind of language that precedes speech. Whoever held out a crust of bread or a can of water to you when you'd already fallen on your knees from sheer weakness—his is a hand you'll never forget.

Wickedness is like generosity: neither needs words. Evil prefers concealment and darkness, and generosity doesn't like to trumpet its own deeds. War is full of suffering and despair. These are extremely difficult feelings that appear to require detailed explanation, but what can one do—the greater the suffering and the more intense the feelings of despair, the more superfluous words become.

It was only after the war that words reappeared. People once again began questioning and wondering, and those who had not been there demanded explanations. The explanations offered seemed pathetic and ridiculous, but the need to explain and to interpret is so deeply ingrained in us that, even if you realize how inadequate such explanations are, this doesn't stop you from trying to make them. Clearly, such attempts were an effort to return to normal civilian life, but unfortunately the effort was ludicrous. Words are powerless when confronted by catastrophe; they're pitiable, wretched, and easily distorted. Even ancient prayers are powerless in the face of disaster.

At the beginning of the 1950s, when I started to write, rivers of words were already flowing about the war. Many recounted, bore witness to, confessed, evaluated. The people who had promised themselves and their dear ones that after the war they would tell everything did indeed keep their promise. That's how the notebooks, the booklets, and the volumes of memoirs all came about. These pages carry a great deal of pain, but there is also within them much that is clichéd and superficial. The silence that had reigned during the war and for a short while afterward seemed to be swallowed up in an ocean of words.

The really huge catastrophes are the ones that we tend to surround with words so as to protect ourselves from them. The first words that I wrote were a kind of desperate cry to find the silence that had enfolded me during the war. A sixth sense told me that my soul was enveloped in this same silence, and that if I managed to revive it perhaps the right words would come.

My writing began with a severe handicap. The experiences of the war lay heavily and oppressively within me, and I wanted to repress them even more. I wanted to build a new life on top of my previous one. It took me years to return to the way I had been, and even when I did, there was still a long way to go. How does one give form to such a searing flame? Where does one start? How does one connect the links? What words does one use?

What had been written about World War II had been mainly testimonies and accounts that had been deemed authentic expressions; literature was considered a fabrication. But I could not simply bear witness. I could not remember the names of people or places—only gloom, rustlings, and movements. Only much later did I understand that this raw material is the very marrow of literature, and that, from it, it's possible to create an interior narrative. I say "interior" because at that time chronicles were considered to be where truth was to be found. "Interior" expression had not yet been born.

My poetics had been formed at the start of my life; by this I mean by everything that I saw and absorbed from my parents' home and throughout the long war. It was then that my attitude toward people, toward beliefs, toward emotions, and toward words was molded. This relationship has not changed over the years. Although my life has become richer, although I've added words, concepts, and knowledge, my basic relationship to the world has not changed. During the war, I saw life naked—plain and unadorned. The good and the bad, the beautiful and the ugly—all these were revealed to me as strands of the same rope. Thank God it didn't turn me into a moralist. On the contrary, I learned how to respect human weakness and how to love it, for weakness is our essence and our humanity. A man who is aware of his weaknesses is far more likely to be able to overcome them. A moralist cannot face his own weaknesses; instead of criticizing himself, he criticizes his neighbor.

I've talked about silence and about suspicion, about preferring fact to explanation. I don't like to talk about emotions. Too much talk about emotions will always lead us into a thicket of sentimentality—to trampling on and flattening true emotions. But emotion that emerges from action is the absolute essence of feeling.

18

I TURN THE PAGES of my old diary. They are a yellowish-green, some have stuck together, and my uneven handwriting is already blurred. For many years the diary lay in a suitcase, unopened. I was afraid of these notebooks, afraid they would reveal fears and character flaws that I've been trying to hide from myself for years.

It is 1946, the year I came to Israel, and the diary is a mosaic of words in German, Yiddish, Hebrew, and even Ruthenian. I say "words" and not "sentences" because in 1946 I was not able to connect words into sentences, and the words were the suppressed cries of a fourteen-year-old youth who'd lost all the languages he had spoken and was now left without language. The diary became a hiding place where he could pile up the remnants of his mother tongue and the words that he had just acquired. A "pile of stuff" is not just a figure of speech; it described my soul.

Without language, everything is chaos and confusion and the fear of things you needn't be afraid of. Without language, one's naked character is exposed. Back then, most of the children around me stuttered, spoke too loudly, or swallowed their words. The extroverts among us spoke too loudly, and as for the introverts, their voices were swallowed up in the silence inside them. Without a mother tongue, a person has a defect.

My mother's native tongue had been German. She loved the language and cultivated it, and when she spoke it, the words had the sound of a crystal bell. My grandmother spoke Yiddish, and her language had a different ring, or, rather, taste to it, for it always brought to my mind plum compote. The maid spoke Ukrainian, with some of our words and some of Grandmother's thrown in, too. I spent many hours with her every day. She wasn't strict with me; all she wanted was to make me happy. I loved her and her language. To this day I carry the memory of her face in me, even though at the crucial moment, when her help was as vital to us as the air we breathed, she fled our house along with our jewelry and cash, which she stashed in the pockets of her dress.

Another language, which we didn't use at home but which was the most common on the streets, was Romanian. After World War I, Bukovina, the country of my birth, was annexed to Romania and the official language became Romanian. We spoke only broken Romanian and never mastered this language.

Four languages surrounded us and lived within us, complementing one another in a strange way. If you were speaking German and you were searching for a word, phrase, or proverb, you'd use Yiddish or Ruthenian. My parents tried, but couldn't maintain the purity of their German, because words from all the languages that surrounded us flowed imperceptibly into our own, insinuating themselves. These four languages merged into one, rich in nuance, contrasts, humor, and satire. This language had lots of room for emotion, for delicate shadings of feeling, imagination, and memory. Today these languages no longer live within me, but I feel their roots. Sometimes, as if by magic, just one word will evoke entire scenes.

I RETURN TO 1946, the year I came to Israel. On the ship and afterward, at the camp at Atlit, where we were interned by the British, we learned some Hebrew words. They sounded exotic but were hard to pronounce. They lacked warmth, their sound aroused no associations, as if they had been born from the sand that surrounded us on all sides. Worse yet, they sounded like orders—Work! Eat! Clean up! Go to sleep!—as if this were a language of soldiers, and not one in which you could converse quietly. On the kibbutzim and in the youth villages, this language was forced upon us. At the very least, those who spoke in their mother tongues would be sternly reprimanded.

I had never been talkative, but now the few words that might have come out of me were swallowed back in. We stopped speaking among ourselves, and, as is the case in any critical situation, basic character traits were laid bare. The extroverts and the bossy knew how to take advantage. They turned their words into orders that quickly filled the vacuum, taking control of the empty space as their voices rang out loudly. I would retreat into myself more and more. My first year in Israel was not an opening out to the world for me, but an even more extreme withdrawal into myself.

During that first year we worked in the fields and we learned Hebrew, the Bible, and the poems of Hayyim Nach-man Bialik. Memories of home and the sounds of its language faded away, but the new language would not take root easily.

There were youths who adopted Hebrew slang as if they'd been born here, the words tripping off their tongues with ease. But for me, for some reason, saying even a single word—let alone a sentence—required a huge effort.

Sometimes I'd go to Jaffa, where a few distant relatives lived—people I'd known before the war. In their midst, my mother tongue would temporarily leave its prison. To overcome my muteness and stuttering, I read widely in the two languages I knew: German and Yiddish. I would repeat entire sentences so as to bring back some fluency.

The effort to preserve my mother tongue amid surroundings that imposed another language upon me proved futile. From week to week it dwindled; by the end of that first year all that remained were embers. The pain this brought was double-edged. My mother had been murdered at the start of the war, and all through it I carried her image within me, somehow believing that I would meet up with her when it was over and things would go back to the way they had been. My mother and her language were one and the same. Now, as that language faded within me, it was as if my mother were dying a second time. A deep sadness suffused me like a drug, not only during my waking hours, but in sleep as well. While asleep, I would be wandering with a convoy of refugees, all of them stuttering, with only the roadside animals—the horses, the cows, and the dogs—speaking fluently, as if man and beast had exchanged places.

The effort to adopt Hebrew and to turn it into my mother tongue continued for some years; the yellowing diary that lies on my desk is enduring testimony to this. It doesn't take a graphologist to note the confusion and disorientation there. Spelling mistakes are no less pronounced in Hebrew than in German. Every letter signals great rupture and sorrow, but not a lack of self-consciousness. *What will become of me without a language?* I ask myself in these faded diaries. *Without a language I'm like a stone.* I don't know where I got that image, but it seems like a good metaphor for the feeling that without a language I would also wither away in an ugly and lengthy desiccation, like the garden behind our dormitory during winter.

My years in the youth village and then in the army were not congenial ones. Some young people did find themselves through agricultural work, quite a few carved out their niche within the regular army, but most of them joined the general labor force, dispersing in all directions. We tended to meet up less and less frequently. Without a language a man doesn't talk. My mother tongue, which I had greatly loved, died within me after two years in Israel. I tried to revive it in different ways, by reading and even repeating words and sentences, but despite these efforts it still died rapidly.

From the moment I arrived in Israel, I hated the people who forced me to speak Hebrew, and with the death of my mother tongue, my hostility toward them only increased. This hostility did not, of course, change the situation, but it did clarify it. Quite obviously, I was neither here nor there. What had been mine—my parents, my home, and my mother tongue—was now lost to me forever, and this language, which promised to be my mother tongue, was nothing more than a stepmother.

Let me be clear: we acquired the rudiments of Hebrew quite quickly, and by the end of first year we could even read the newspaper. But there was little joy in this acquisition. It was like being trapped in a protracted military tour of duty that would last for many years and for which I immediately had to adopt the soldiers' language. But at the end of my service (which would be equivalent to the end of the war), I would return to my mother tongue. There was, of course, an inescapable dilemma: that language had been German—the language of those who murdered my mother. How does one go back to speaking in a language drenched in the blood of Jews? This dilemma, in all its severity, did not detract from the feeling that my German was not the language of those Germans but the language of my mother, and it was as clear as daylight that if I met up with her I'd speak to her in the language that we had spoken together since I was a small child.

My years in the army were years of loneliness and estrangement. I had no home in Israel, and being posted in the desolate huts in Tzrifin, at Beit Lid, and at Hazerim, doing guard duty day and night, only increased this sense of alienation. Because I had nowhere to escape to, I escaped into my diary. The entries from those days are full of longing for my parents and for the home I had lost. It's strange that, of all places, it was in the army that my first stutterings should have taken the shape of short poems. I say "poems," but they were more like the howling of an abandoned animal who takes up his cries time and again with a wearying monotony. Thoughts, feelings, and images churned within me all the time, but without words everything shrank to a mere whimper.

In the army I started to read Hebrew literature, or, more accurately, I tried to do so. It was like a sheer mountain wall, and climbing it was far beyond my capabilities. In the early 1950s, S. Yizhar and Moshe Shamir were the writers in vogue. Every page was a hurdle for me, and yet I still read voraciously, as if trying to familiarize myself with the strange country into which I had been thrown. At the same time, I searched for myself and my identity in young characters with a similar fate. But what I got from the pages I read was a strange world, populated by young people who were set in their views, soldiers or officers or farmers in the open fields. Though the life I had come from lacked structure or dignity, neither did it have childish naïveté or idealization. I went back and read, but the more I read, the clearer it became that this beautiful and honest life of work, warfare, and love would not be my allotted portion, even if I were to accomplish the impossible.

Another matter, but in fact the same thing: during that period people around me all seemed to speak in very elevated words and in slogans. From my childhood I've hated pomposity, preferring instead small, quiet words that evoke scents and sounds. Here again was a conflict that there was no bridging.

In time it became clear to me that I needed to have a different connection to Hebrew, not an external connection but an interior one. In this, as in other areas, people came to my aid, and it is doubtful whether without their help I would have been able to leave the prison in which I found myself. First and foremost were Dov Sadan and, later, Leib Roichman. I learned Yiddish with Dov Sadan. Yiddish had been the language of my grandparents. During the war and my subsequent wanderings, my Yiddish vocabulary increased, but I never arrived at a real grasp of the language. For Sadan, Yiddish and Hebrew dwelt side by side, like twin sisters. In his classes we spoke Hebrew, but we read the texts in Yiddish. From Sadan, I learned something that was not much talked about in those days: that most Hebrew writers were bilingual, that they wrote simultaneously in the two languages. This was a sensational discovery for me. It meant that the "here" and the "there" were not cut off from each other, as the slogans proclaimed. We read Mendele Mocher Sefarim in his two languages, and Bialik, Steinberg, and Agnon. Their Hebrew was connected to places with which I was familiar, to landscapes I remembered, and to forgotten melodies that came to me from my grandparents' prayers. The Hebrew of my youth-village days and of the army had been a language unto itself, unconnected to my previous language or life experience.

Dov Sadan laid out another kind of Jewish map before us, a map in which Hebrew and Yiddish, the art of a people and the art of individuals, coexisted. In Sadan's inclusive vision, there was no monolithic Jewishness, neither linguistic nor artistic. He saw contemporary Jewish life as though after a catastrophic rupture, to use a Kabbalistic term. He believed that then, as now, there were many fragments of Jewish life that had splintered off from that rupture, and that it was our job to reconnect them, drawing out the sparks of holiness hidden within them all and bringing them together. He real-ized that the major Jewish movements of the past two hun-dred years—Hasidism, its Lithuanian opponents, the Jewish Enlightenment, and the national Jewish rebirth—no longer had the power to exist separately, and that a new Jewish life had to be created from them. This pluralism sounded strange back then. Ideologues couldn't stand pluralism. Their world was divided into black and white: the Diaspora versus the Homeland, commerce versus a life of labor, collective life ver-sus private life. And above everything hovered the familiar slogan: "Forget the Diaspora and root yourself in the present!"

But what could I do? Within me there was a deep refusal to efface my past and build a new life on its ruins. The idea that a person has to destroy his past in order to build a new life seemed to me totally misguided even then, but I didn't dare voice this thought, not even to myself. On the contrary, I blamed myself for having a Diaspora mentality, for having a bourgeois outlook, and, of course, for hopeless egotism. In this respect, Sadan was a true guide for me. He knew exactly where I had come from and the legacy I bore blindly within me, and he also guessed that in the future it would form the foundation and the building blocks of my life.

Leib Roichman was a Yiddish writer, someone with whom I became very close. At his home I heard a different

kind of Yiddish. A small group of us would get together frequently, and he would read aloud from Yiddish poetry and
prose. It was at his home that I heard the poems of M. L.
Halperin, Ya'akov Glattstein, and Rachel Zichlinski for the
first time. He read quietly and without dramatization, as if he
were pouring the words into us.

Roichman had grown up in a Hasidic household and
been educated at the home of the Rabbi of Prusof. Unlike
other members of his generation, he kept faith with his
Hasidic heritage. His vocabulary and his expressions were
completely Hasidic, although his lifestyle was not. Once a
week I would sit with him and read the Hasidic classics, such
as *Likutei Maharan*. The books were written in Hebrew, but
not in modern spoken Hebrew—certainly not the Hebrew I
knew from the youth movement. "Work" meant worshipping
God, "providence" meant Divine Providence, "security" was
not the defense of small villages but the security of faith in
God. Not only did the words have different meanings, but the
sentences did, too. It was as if they were being played to a different tune, a kind of blend of Yiddish and Hebrew, with an
occasional Slavic word thrown in here and there.

Though Yiddish literature and Hasidic literature were
in complete contrast to everything that was then going on in
Israel, for me these two aspects of my life were pleasantly
compatible, just as they'd been in the home I had lost. But I
sensed something that only later did I come to understand in
greater depth: literature, if it is genuine, is the religious
melody that has been lost to us. Literature gathers within it all
the elements of faith: the seriousness, the internality, the
melody, and the connection with the hidden aspects of the
soul. It goes without saying how far this concept was from
the ubiquitous social realism then rampant in the socialist
newspapers. In truth, even I wasn't quite aware in those days

of what I was learning from my two teachers, or where these studies would lead me over time.

When I look through my diary from the late 1940s and the early 1950s, there is a clear division. When I write about my parents' home, most of the words are in German or in Yiddish; when I speak of my life in Israel, the words are in Hebrew. Not until the mid-1950s do the sentences begin to flow consistently, and in Hebrew. Adopting the language was simpler for the friends who had come to Israel with me, because they cut themselves off from memory and built themselves a language that was completely "here," and here alone. From this perspective, they were the faithful sons of that era. We had come to Israel, as the saying went, "to build and to be rebuilt." This was interpreted by most of us as the extinction of memory, a complete personal transformation and a total identification with this narrow strip of land. In other words, we had come to Israel to "lead a normal life"—as such terms used to be defined.

My diary is stuttering and impoverished, and yet, at the same time, it is full to bursting. What it does not have is longing, guilt, sketches that are drawn from observation, or sexual yearning. Beyond all this, there's a desperate attempt to connect precious childhood memories with a new life. This was a perpetual struggle, one that was waged across a broad front and included: my education, which had terminated in the first grade; my puny body and low self-esteem; a memory that had been commanded to forget but refused to do so; and the ideological complacency that sought to make me into a man of narrow horizons, which I refused to be. In another way, this struggle was also to safeguard that core of myself that was being asked to be something he didn't want to be and couldn't be. But above all, I fought to acquire the language and to adopt it as my own tongue. At a very early age, and before I knew that fate would push me toward literature, instinct whispered that without an intimate knowledge of language my life would be superficial and impoverished.

The attitude at that time regarding language was overwhelmingly functional: "Build up your vocabulary and you've got a language!" This approach tried to uproot you from your world and implant you in a world you could barely grasp. One must admit that, on the whole, it succeeded, but, alas, at what price—a memory that had been eradicated and a soul that had been reduced to superficiality.

19

BETWEEN THE YEARS 1946 AND 1948, I was in the Aliyat Hano'ar Youth Movement, and between 1948 and 1950, I was an apprentice at the agricultural school founded by Rachel Yana'it at Ein Kerem, on the outskirts of Jerusalem. After that, I attended the Hannah Meizel Agricultural School, in Nahalal, in the valley of Emeq Yizre'el. For four straight years, I lived close to the earth, certain that I was fated to become a farmer. I loved the earth and, in particular, the trees that I took care of. During those years, my days had a simple routine: rising at dawn, intensive work from 6 a.m. to 8 a.m., a full and savory breakfast, and, after that, a long stretch of work. I loved the afternoon nap on hot summer days. In those years, part of me was, indeed, numb. The war had settled inside me like a stone, and I grew increasingly close to the earth, to the Hebrew language, and to the books I was reading with great thirst. To be as faithful as possible to those far-off years, I'll quote some passages from my diary just as they were written (apart from the correction of some very minor grammatical and spelling mistakes).

DECEMBER 30, 1946

Today I learned the art of pruning. Sometimes it seems to me that I haven't come here, but was born here. I love the earth and the trees so much that it's hard to describe it as a new love. Were it at all possible to erase the war years from my soul completely, I would blend in more easily with the earth—there would be no barrier between us.

JANUARY 17, 1947

Today there was a military call-up, and so I was assigned to the vegetable garden. This work requires many people. Annuals make me despair. You plant them and almost immediately you have to pull them up. In an orchard you care for trees over several years: you delight in their growth, in their new life each season. "For man is like a tree of the field," I read in the Bible. Only a man who plants trees can understand this.

ANOTHER ENTRY, UNDATED

Today I picked Santa Rosa plums, and it was good that I was alone. Working with lots of people confuses me, and, even worse, I cease to feel and to think. Only when I'm truly alone do I connect with the earth and grow inside.

AND ON THE SAME PAGE

During the morning break, the instructor, M., asked me casually where I'd been during the war. The question so surprised me that I stood there open-mouthed. "Many places," I recovered sufficiently to say, and looked for an excuse to escape further questioning. For some reason, M. did not let the matter rest, and I felt trapped, caught. And mute. A great anxiety gripped me, and my memory shut down. I didn't know what to answer, so I repeated, "In many places."

Every night I tell myself: Forget more and more. The more I forget, the easier it will be to blend in with the earth and with the language. There are many obstacles. Last night I had a long talk with the instructor S. We spoke German. It's been years since I've spoken German, and yet I still spoke it fluently. It seems that it's impossible to uproot one's mother tongue.

I had this dream: Mother, Father, and I are bathing on the banks of the Prut. Two long barges pass in front of us. Mother and Father are so young that they look more like high-school students than parents. For a moment I'm amazed at their transformation. Mother gives me a hug and says, "It's a masked ball, soon everything will be as it was."

The morning reveille shattered my dream.

Last night, there was a lecture in the dining room. A middle-aged man wearing a blue shirt spoke about the Jewish "weakness" and praised the partisans and the illegal immigrants who make their way to Israel, and decried the black marketeers ensconcing themselves in Jaffa and Tel Aviv. "We must change!" he urged us. "We must become farmers and fighters." While I found myself identifying with his words, I was put off by him. He seemed like the sort of man who would not hesitate to use physical violence. Let's hope I am wrong.

In dreams I'm still on the road, being pursued and falling into deep pits. Last night, one of my pursuers grabbed me by the ankle and pulled me into a deep pit. I plunged in. It was a relief to awaken and find I was unharmed.

IN MY NAÏVETÉ I believed that my previous life had died within me and what was going on inside me was no more than the last gasps of visions of the past. During most of the day-light hours I would be outside, plowing, harrowing, pruning, or grafting in the nursery. This way of life seemed to me so real, so right, that anything else seemed external, or irrelevant. In those days I harbored another feeling, which had been implanted in me in my grandfather's home in the country, and at times in the forest, when I lived there alone—something like a religious sensibility.

I come from an assimilated home that had not a trace of religious belief. There was plenty of serenity and attentiveness, and we all treated one another with sensitivity—but it was all done on a rational basis. Formal religion was thought to lack real feeling; it was considered vulgar and ill conceived. This, apparently, was due more to the *Zeitgeist* than to personal experience, for my mother's mother kept her religious feelings hidden and displayed no obvious affectations. Grandfather loved Mother very much, and I never heard him preach to her or try to coerce her, even though he knew that our urban lifestyle was far from kosher. I knew—or, more exactly, I often felt—that my mother harbored a hidden affection for the faith of her forefathers, even though this affection was never tangibly expressed. Moreover, at home we carefully avoided words that might be construed as expressing belief. All such expressions of belief were dubbed *magia*, or hocus-pocus.

I loved Grandfather and Grandmother's village, their spacious wooden house, the acacia trees growing next to it, the orchard, the rows of vegetables in the garden, and even the toilet that was outside the house, a kind of little wooden outhouse covered in ivy. There was mystery in everything. It was not surprising that I felt that God dwells only in the countryside. In the village I would walk with Grandfather to the synagogue, listen to the prayers, and gaze at the wooden lions above the Ark that housed the Torah scrolls. In the vil-

lage God dwelt in every shady corner and under the heavy
boughs of the acacia trees. In my heart I was sometimes
amazed that Mother and Father didn't see what was so clear to
me and to Grandfather.

Later, when I escaped from the camp and lived in the
forest, this sense of mystery came back to me. I was certain
that God would save me and return me to my parents. If truth
be told, throughout the war my parents were mixed up in my
mind with God, as a kind of heavenly choir, accompanied by
angels, that was supposed to come and save me from my
wretched existence.

These visions faded away at the end of the war, when I
found myself crammed in among masses of other refugees.
During most of the war, I had been by myself and hadn't spoken to anyone. I'd been sustained by visions and fantasies.
Sometimes I would give myself up to them and forget that I
was in danger.

My days in the youth movement were hard for me
because, among other things, I was suddenly surrounded by
children of my own age and I was forced to speak. Both the
presence of those children and the need to speak were in fact
so hard for me that on more than one occasion I was ready to
run away. My diary from the years 1946 to 1950 is full of longing for the days when I had been alone, surrounded by trees
and vistas and living a silent life that didn't impose speech
on me.

The time I spent in the forest and with the peasants had
compelled me to be silent and alert. Had I grown up in my
home, I suppose I would have developed a normal flow of
speech. My parents didn't talk a lot, but there was a culture of
conversation at home. My parents were sensitive to language,
and I would often hear them discussing the meaning of a word
or a phrase. During the war, when I was forced to hide my

identity, the first rule was silence. After the war, when people saw that no sounds issued from my mouth, they assumed that I was mute. By then I really was almost mute.

The years 1946 to 1950 were years of verbiage; when life is full of ideology, words and clichés abound. Everyone talked. Sometimes it seemed to me that everyone had attended a school for preachers—only I hadn't studied there. Not only did people chatter away in the home, in the street, and at meetings, but the literature of the period was also full of excess verbiage. The literary writing overflowed with words. It seemed as though you could not read a book without having a dictionary right next to you, as was the case with the works of S. Yizhar and Moshe Shamir, among others. My diary is full of admiration for these stacks of words and descriptions; I was certain that I would never be able to write correctly.

Someone who finds it difficult to talk needs a diary. When I look through my diary, I discover that it's full of unfinished sentences and an obsession with precision. More than the words themselves, the gaps between them are elo-quent. At any rate, my diary is not a text that flows easily, but, rather, a mode of expression that is full of inhibitions. I say this without looking for excuses, but to understand my own process of maturation.

My early writing was more about holding back than about flowing; it was a sort of continuation of the diary. Some-thing of my way of speaking clung to it. The perpetual fear that something flawed would slip out and betray me, so typical of the way I spoke even years after the war, also found expres-sion in my early writing. None of my attempts to improve the flow helped. My writing was like walking on tiptoe—distrustful and hesitant.

During the 1950s, I wrote little, and what I wrote I would then ruthlessly erase. I turned the tendency to use words sparingly into a golden rule. In those years, books were brimming with descriptions of landscapes and people. "He paints on a broad canvas," people would say approvingly. What was broad was considered epic. The first rejection letters I received from editors said simply, You have to fill it out, you have to expand, the picture isn't there yet. There's no doubt that my writing during this period was full of flaws, but not for the reasons that these editors cited.

During the late 1950s, I gave up my ambition to become an Israeli writer and made every effort to become what I really was: an émigré, a refugee, a man who carries within him the child of war, who finds talking difficult and tries to speak with a minimum amount of words. This effort culminated in my first book, *Smoke*, which appeared in 1962.

Many editors paged through the manuscript before I found a publisher. Every one found a different flaw. One claimed that you shouldn't write imaginatively about the Holocaust; by contrast, another contended that you shouldn't write about the weaknesses of the victims but should emphasize the heroism, the ghetto uprisings, and the partisans. Some claimed that my style itself was flawed, not "normative," meager. And for some reason, all of them wanted to make corrections—to add something or to take something away. These editors overlooked the book's virtues and its authenticity. As a result, I also couldn't see these qualities; furthermore, I was convinced that everything I was told was true. It's strange with what ease we adopt criticism. Criticism that originates from within oneself can be destructive, but there's nothing as destructive as criticism that comes from others. It took me years to free myself from this and to understand that I, and I alone, can best steer my course.

Smoke was, however, favorably received. Critics said things like, "Appelfeld doesn't write on the Holocaust but about its margins. He isn't sentimental, he's restrained." That was considered a compliment, and I was happy about it. However, even then I was labeled a "Holocaust writer." There is nothing more annoying. A writer, if he's a *writer*, writes from within himself and mainly about himself, and if there is any meaning to what he says, it's because he's faithful to himself—to his voice and his rhythm. Theme, subject matter—all these are by-products of his writing, not its essence. I was a child during the war. This child grew up, and all that happened to him and within him continued into his adulthood: the loss of his home, the loss of his language, suspicion, fear, the inhibitions of speech, the feelings of alienation in a foreign country. It was from these that I wove my fiction. Only the right words can construct a literary text, not subject matter.

I do not pretend to be a messenger, a chronicler of the war, or a know-it-all. I feel attached to the places I have lived in, and I write about them. I don't feel that I write about the past. Pure and unadulterated, the past is no more than good raw material for literature. Literature is an enduring present—not in a journalistic sense, but as an attempt to bring time into an ongoing present.

20

AT THE AGE of eighteen, I still couldn't write properly. At the army induction center in Afula, standing half naked by the door of a room where the medical committee was to examine me, I filled out a form and the clerk corrected two spelling mistakes in it. It was not the first time this had happened. Whenever I was corrected, I'd feel slightly wounded. It seemed to me that I would never know how to write, and that there would always be someone who'd find mistakes in my writing.

I was then asked to take off my undershirt. The three doctors stared at me as I stood before them. They were different from the doctors that I remembered from home. One of them approached me, checked my pulse and my blood pressure, and asked me to get up on the scale and to give him my glasses. The other two doctors also checked my glasses and their thick lenses.

I stood there while they consulted in whispers. It seemed to me they were commenting on how skinny I was, on my poor eyesight, and on the curvature in my back. Although they whispered, it seemed to me they wanted me to hear.

"Have you had any illnesses?" I was asked.

"Typhus," I replied immediately.

Anyone who'd been in the camps had contracted typhus. It was also a sign of the approaching end. Children lasted only a few days, as they curled up and faded away.

"Where and when were you born?" Always the same question.

"Czernowitz, 1932."

"Your parents' names?"

"My mother was Bonia and my father, Michael."

"Elementary school?"

"First grade."

"High school?"

"No."

These frequently asked questions now seemed to resonate all the more, as if they were revealing something for the first time.

The doctors again looked hard at me, and one of them asked, "When did you come to Israel?"

"In 1946."

"And what have you been doing?"

"Two years in the Aliyat Hano'ar Youth Movement, and two years' apprenticeship in the orchards."

"Do you want to serve in the army?"

"Yes."

For some reason, this made all three of them chuckle.

"Get dressed," I was ordered.

My nakedness and the questions that I was asked made me uneasy. It seemed to me that serious flaws in my body and my state of mind had just been found, and that I would soon be told that I couldn't serve in the army. I was sure that the announcement would be accompanied by severe condemnation.

I looked at them again. They were speaking among themselves. I understood nothing of what they were saying, but the thought that they were talking about me in secrecy increased my anxiety.

"And did you have any brothers or sisters?"

"No."

For a moment it seemed to me that they were trying to solve a riddle. The riddle was me, and they lacked only a few details, but soon the complete condemnation would be announced.

I'm healthy, I was about to say. *My shortsightedness doesn't prevent me from reading. It's important for me to serve in a fighting unit. Being placed in a fighting unit would do away with all the injuries and insults that I have sustained. I'm sure I'll be able to handle any mission I'm given. Just let me have the chance to prove it.* While I was still preoccupied with these thoughts, the doctor who'd checked me lifted his head from his papers and declared, "Fit for service," as if he'd finally solved the riddle.

Fit for service, but not for fighting.

In the months before the exam, I had made a huge effort to toughen up, or, more accurately, to appear tougher. I ran, I worked out, I climbed hills, and I lifted weights. Perhaps because of all this, I lost weight. Not for nothing did they ask if I ate well. I trained because I wanted to be accepted into a fighting unit. The notion that one day I'd be a regular soldier alongside other soldiers, or perhaps even an officer, took up a great deal of my thoughts. It seemed to me that the army framework—the training and the actual combat—would change not only my body but my character as well. The sensitivity that had caused me such suffering would disappear, and I would become tall and rugged. I would look like a soldier.

Now this dream was gone. The army did take me, but on a very restricted basis: Fit for Service. An "FFS" is really half a soldier, or even a quarter of a soldier—one who serves those in active combat, supplies their uniforms, feeds them, but is never one of them.

We all stood outside in the sun and waited for the truck that would take us to the camp for basic training. The noncombatants were grouped in one corner, and the fighters stood next to a eucalyptus tree. One had to admit that the difference was striking. The fighters were taller, and attractively self-confident. They spoke in rough voices, were better built, and were even hairier. The noncombatants gave themselves away by their mannerisms, which were slack and sloppy. But beyond these mannerisms was what the eyes revealed: there was no sparkle to them, no fire of determination. A dullness appeared there instead. It was clear: the FFSs hadn't been born to heroic deeds; they were going to sit out their time on bases in the rear and serve the soldiers who were destined for heroism. I was full of regret that fate couldn't have prepared something better for me. Henceforth the division was clear: some of us for dazzling deeds and some for dull service. It took me no time at all to see that those who had been called up with me knew one another. Most were local, from Afula, and had studied together in grade school and in high school. I was the only foreigner, an outsider, carrying within me the landscapes of a foreign country, another language, and experiences about which I was unable to speak.

A soldier came up to me. "What's your name?" he asked.

I told him.

"Where did you go to school?"

"I didn't go to school."

"You must be joking."

The young man looked at me with a mixture of pity and scorn. I knew that I had come to a crossroads, but it wasn't within my power to change anything. A soft body and lack of education are handicaps everywhere. In the army they determine everything. I tried for some time to get accepted into various training programs, but nothing came of it. All doors were closed to me.

At the induction center I met S., a recruit who, unlike me, had spent the war with his parents in hiding in a Belgian village. During the long years of the war, his parents had taught him everything that's studied in high school, and more. His father was a famous linguist, his mother a scientist. For S., the war years were years of intensive study. In addition to French, he spoke German, English, and apparently other languages, too. His very appearance indicated that he was talented and studious. He was tall and fragile-looking, and his long fingers hinted at a certain refinement and sensitivity. He spoke to me in my mother tongue, German, and his phrases were elegant, chosen from a broad vocabulary. I didn't understand all of it. That was how my family had spoken, but because of the war, I had lost everything. Even words I once knew had been forgotten.

I was with S. throughout basic training. It was from him that I first heard names like Kafka, Sartre, and Camus, and words such as "intensive," "dramatic," and "integral." He was always talking about famous people, historic places, and, of course, books.

"And you studied throughout the entire war?" I would ask him, unable to restrain myself.

"I studied and I was tested."

"Who tested you?"

"My father."

S. was pleasant, but at the same time there was something frightening about him, as if he were of an altogether different breed. Basic training was not easy for him, either, but he always had some ironic response, some sarcastic comment that made light of the sergeant major's shouts. Though his parents had not equipped him with a strong body, they had given him an abundance of words, which protected him and helped him along when he carried mortars or ammunition. His irony and contempt, though not directed at me, hurt me nonetheless.

I was jealous of S. Of all the languages that I had spoken at home, there was not even one in which I was still fluent. The books that I remembered were those of Jules Verne, but, if truth be told, I had forgotten them, too.

I made no friends during basic training, and S. was the only person with whom I spoke. One could see that the war years had somehow passed him by, and had only broadened his knowledge. He had studied and he had absorbed what he had studied. He was always sprinkling his conversation with French or English words. Had it not been for the war, I would have been like S., but I had spent the war in a ghetto, in a camp, and on the Ukrainian steppes. Even if I were to devote the rest of my life to studying, I would never be able to attain S.'s level of erudition.

"And were you really in hiding for all the years of the war?" I couldn't keep the envy out of my voice.

"Correct."

"And you never left the hiding place?"

"At night we would go upstairs to the living room."

"And you had food?"

"Plenty of it."

There was no doubt about it: S. would emerge victorious from any war. His frail body was full of confidence, belief in himself, and scorn for an army that had placed him in such

21

MY DIARY FOR 1950 TO 1952, my years of army service, is almost empty. During that time, I did not have so
much as a corner I could call my own, and the diary reflects
this. In the army, and in particular during the long stretches of
waiting, I would read anything that came to hand. I say that I
"read," but it would be more accurate to say that I devoured—
quite indiscriminately, as if I was trying to catch up on all I
had missed. There was no getting around it: my lack of education pained me.

It was not, however, from books that I drew knowledge
and understanding, but from life itself. I had been placed
within the rigid environment of the army: inspections morning and evening, rules about our appearance, about how our
beds were to be made up, and about how to clean and maintain our rifles. I had known suffering in the ghetto and in the
camp, but the suffering I experienced in the army was different: it was not from hunger and thirst, but from emotional
pressure. In the army I was like an animal that attempts to

make itself as small as possible, to disguise itself, to sneak away, or to disappear. I experienced the kind of secret relish felt by those who have tiptoed around the rim of an abyss without falling into it. In this hidden delight was the triumph of the weak.

I was now eighteen years old and slightly clumsy. The uniform that was meant to fill me with pride somehow failed to do so. On the contrary, I felt trapped and constricted. In the early 1950s, the army was strict and inflexible. After years of underground activity, it wanted to be recognized as a regular military force, just like any other. As is the case with all revolutions, this was carried to the extreme. Humiliation and arbitrary behavior came along with discipline. I suffered from the confinement and the coercion, and to overcome my distress, I adopted a stratagem familiar to me from my childhood: close-range observation.

There are a few noteworthy aspects of observation: when you observe, you're on the outside, a little higher up, and distant. From this perspective you can understand that whoever's shouting at you is perhaps really shouting at his father or his mother. It's only by chance that you've crossed his path. But a person who doesn't shout can sometimes be worse than one who does. To curry favor with his superiors, he drags us out on night marches and orders us to dig square holes—all just to prove to his superior officer that his company isn't idling about. Obsequious people tend to grovel, and, to my surprise, I discovered they have certain telltale characteristics: in the army, they tended to be overweight and, despite their youth, already padded with quite a layer of fat. Through observation, you can shake off some of your sadness and self-pity. The more you observe, the less pain you feel.

Even as a child, I loved to observe. For hours I would sit

by the double-glazed window and watch the falling snow. In summer I would sit in the garden, looking at the flowers and watching the pets stretched out in the yard. Observation always brought me pleasure—the pleasure of blending in with whatever I was looking at. Only later, at age six or seven, did I start paying attention to form and detail. For example, I noticed that our neighbor's cat wore a pink ribbon, and our neighbor herself—not a tall woman and curvaceously plump—wore a long dress with a deep décolletage and a ribbon in her hair that was very similar to the one worn around the neck of her cat. She wasn't married, but she had a lover, an officer in the Romanian army who visited her every night. He had spurs on his boots, which meant that he was in the cavalry.

Ours was a two-family house. Our master bedroom abutted her master bedroom, and our bathroom was next to her bathroom. She spent much of the day in her bathroom, primping and perfuming herself for her lover's visit that night. When she walked out the front door, wearing a rose-pink gown and a ribbon in her hair, she reeked of heavy perfume. Mother couldn't stand her, but I actually loved watching her. Like an actress, she changed her dress almost every hour, but her most resplendent clothes were kept for the night. She resembled an animal, but I'm not sure which one. Her lover had the gait of a stallion, and when he went up the stairs, I half expected to hear a neigh.

Our neighbor and her lover are among the most detailed images that remain in my memory: her softness, the couches and the sofas that she plumped with scores of cushions, the heavy rugs, the candles stuck into china saucers, the walls on which were hung oil paintings filled with angels. Our home, by contrast, seemed gloomy and monastic to me, and lacking in decoration. Had it not been for some sketches that

Mother had bought after great deliberation, the walls would have been almost completely bare.

This was how we lived—side by side. We knew her daily schedule and she knew ours. Sometimes she would ask me if I was bored. "I'm never bored," I would truthfully reply, and she would look surprised. When we were being expelled from our house and sent to the ghetto, she stood in her doorway holding her cat, staring at us as if they weren't sending us to our deaths, but as if we had somehow taken leave of our senses.

Then came the hungry days of the ghetto, already without Mother and only with Father, who for most of the day was worked like a slave. Our neighbors, the pharmacist Stein and the accountant Feingold, had for some reason not been conscripted for labor, and they were always pushing to the front wherever food was being distributed. These respectable people had changed beyond recognition. Father was angry with them, but I would simply stand and contemplate them. The time they spent in the ghetto had really changed them. Their narrow faces grew broader, and a strange ruddiness bloomed on their cheeks. They became ghetto animals, undeterred by anything. Father's tendency was always sentimental, in Schiller's sense. If he didn't like something, he would condemn it or get rid of it. Father hated the ugly, the warped, and the immoral. He considered mere observation of these things to be a sign of acquiescence to them, of in some way countenancing or even finding pleasure in them. To him, contemplation meant not taking a firm stand. A man is judged by his deeds, not by his thoughts; that was the rule according to which Father lived. He refused to accept reality with equanimity. He always wanted to correct things or, at the very least, to improve them.

I must have inherited the tendency toward contemplation from my mother. She loved to observe. I would often find her standing by the window, completely lost in thought. It was hard to know if she was gazing at the landscape that could be seen from our window or if she was listening to something that came from within her soul. Never did I find her scrutinizing people. She would make distinctions, and often very subtle ones, as regards the appearance of one person, or the posture of someone else, but she would never stare directly at people. She considered staring to be intrusive, an invasion of someone else's privacy.

As a child during the hungry days of the ghetto, when I was already on my own, I would sit for hours on the steps of abandoned buildings, or next to puddles, or in the town square with the elderly, just gazing at a triangular balcony, at an old man who suddenly shook his cane and struck a dog, or at a woman sitting and playing cards by herself. Observation always gave me the pleasant sense of being immersed in myself. An hour of observation doesn't bring one new ideas. It does, however, fill you with colors, sounds, and rhythm. Sometimes an hour of contemplation provides you with a reservoir of feelings that will last for many days. Genuine observation, like music, is devoid of substantive content.

I was eight years old during the time I spent in the ghetto, and I didn't think about things much; if I thought at all, it was about immediate necessities. I would sit, observing, for hours. The sights flowed toward me and filled me with happiness. At night, what I'd seen during the day would loom enormous and frightening. On one of the last days I spent in the ghetto, I was sitting in the town square and gazing at a group of elderly people who were warming themselves in the sun. All of a sudden one of them got up, came over to me, and gave me a slap on the cheek. I was so astonished that I didn't stir. And he, seeing that I didn't move, slapped me again and shouted, "Now you won't stare anymore. Now you'll know you shouldn't stare."

These unexpected slaps were a step in the budding of my consciousness. For now I knew: observation was not just a matter between me and myself; it also affected other people, and perhaps even hurt them. "Now you won't stare anymore." The words echoed within me, as if I had been caught stealing or cheating. Up to then I had been unaware of my secret passion for observation.

This kind of intense desire is not quenched by a mere slap on the cheek. But since receiving those slaps, I have lost the ability to observe spontaneously, to stand right next to something, contemplate it, and absorb it—sometimes for hours on end. From then on, opportunities for observation had to be snatched and stolen. To overcome my fear, I adopted another stratagem: I began to eavesdrop. But when you eavesdrop you can only picture the face of the person, whether he's tall or short, pleasant or bad. If before that time observation had been one of my sources of happiness, now the happiness became mingled with a sense of sin.

I RETURN TO my days in the army, a difficult time for me. I had already been in Israel for four years, and yet everything was still confusing. The languages that I had brought with me were steadily receding, but I was far from fluent in the Hebrew that I had acquired with so much effort. Harder than this, however, was not having a sense of belonging: living in a country where it was always summer, and stuck in those long barracks during basic training—who was I, and what was I? Although there were quite a few new immigrants among those who had enlisted with me, they seemed to be more involved in what was going on, and, more important, they were stronger than I was. The war years were still coiled within me, and army life seemed to be a continuation of those years, though somewhat transformed: instead of fearing the forest or the Ruthenian peasants who might suddenly recognize me as a Jewish child, there came another fear: the fear of the sergeant major who made my life miserable day and night.

I survived the war not because I was strong or because I had fought for my existence. I was more like a small animal that had found a temporary shelter in a burrow, that fed on whatever it chanced upon. Danger made me into a child who was attentive to his surroundings, but not into a strong child. I would sit for hours in the forest and observe the underbrush, or sit by the side of a stream and watch the current. Contemplation made me forget about the hunger and the fear, and visions of home would return to me. These hours were perhaps the most joyful ones, if one can use this description to describe life during a war. The little boy who was on the verge of getting lost—or even killed—in that savage foreign land could go back to being the child of his father and his mother: walking with them along summer streets, an ice-cream cone in his hand, or swimming with them in the River Prut. These hours of grace preserved me from spiritual extinction at the time, and afterward as well, when I traveled through Europe after the war and during my years in the youth village. I would sit in contemplation, wrapping myself in sights and sounds, connecting with my previous life, and feeling happy not to be just another one of the anonymous thousands who surrounded me.

In the army I was suddenly deprived of this quiet, secret experience. I did not have so much as an hour to myself. To stave off my misery, I learned how to be contemplative even when in the midst of a bustling crowd. It was not the kind of contemplation that awakens one's soul, brings happiness, or expands the mind, but it was a highly practical form of observation: who's good and who's bad, who's selfish and who's generous.

During my army service, I learned to what extent the

experiences of my childhood in the ghetto and in the camp had been ingrained in me. At the youth village there were the written and unwritten watchwords: "forget," "set down roots," "speak Hebrew," "improve your appearance," "cultivate your masculinity." These messages did their work. Anyone who internalized them, adopted them, and lived by them found army life easier. But with me it was quite the opposite: during my service, visions of the ghetto and memories of the camp resurfaced, perhaps because I once again found myself enclosed and threatened. I envied my friends who had also come from the camps; it seemed as though their memories had been erased. It was as if they were free of the past and rooted in this new reality, relishing the food and the sunshine, even the daily and nightly army maneuvers. But for me, as if deliberately to spite me, my time in the ghetto and in the camp seemed to become clearer, and more tangible. If, for a while during my years in the youth village, it seemed that the past was dead and buried, during my army service images that I hadn't seen for years were brought to the surface. To my astonishment, these events were absolutely clear, as if they had taken place yesterday and not earlier.

The army didn't toughen me up. On the contrary, it only intensified my contemplative tendencies. When you are engaged in contemplation, you retreat from yourself, you envelop yourself in a melody that rises up from inside you. You build yourself a shelter, or sometimes elevate yourself, in order to observe from afar. At the time I didn't yet know that this contemplation was quietly equipping me for the role that fate had intended for me.

I learned that a person sees only what he has already been shown. In the ghetto and in the camp I saw people at their lowest levels. I saw untrammeled selfishness, but, again, I also saw tremendous generosity. True, selfishness was more frequent and generosity rarer, but what have in fact been engraved into my memory are those moments of clarity and humanity, when a doomed man was able to set aside his petty and narrow self-interest and sacrifice himself for another. Such rare moments not only showed that man is better than a lowly insect—they also brought some light into the darkness.

During my army service, I met many generous soldiers who helped me. I lost my canteen and would have been put on trial for loss of equipment but for an anonymous soldier who came by and handed me another one. My last pennies had been spent, and I had no money to buy a pack of cigarettes, when another soldier came by and offered me a banknote. In those years there was no one I was close to in Israel, but these good people appeared on just those occasions when despair might have engulfed me.

I made a survey and a reckoning: every person I knew who was saved during the war was saved solely by the grace of someone who, at a time of great danger, extended a hand to him. It was not God that we saw in the camps, but good people. The old Jewish saying that the world continues to exist only by virtue of a few righteous people is as true today as it was back then.

My army service was important for me not because it forged my character or instilled in me new values, but because it led me back to that which was the source of my life. The life that I had lost during the war and my memory of it had begun to disappear, but it was in the army that it came alive, and it was in the army that I came to understand that the world I had left behind—parents, home, street, and city—was alive within me. Everything that had happened to me or that was about to happen to me was connected to the world from which I had sprung. The moment I realized this, I ceased being an orphan dragging his orphanhood behind him and became someone who was able to confront the world.

22

THERE ARE DEMONS everywhere, but in some places they can be seen. During one of my army leaves, I was accosted by a man who claimed that I had done him an injustice after the war.

"In what way?" I asked. I tried to defend myself. "When the war broke out I was seven years old, and when it ended I was barely thirteen."

"Age is irrelevant."

"What are you accusing me of?"

"I shouldn't have to tell you, you know exactly what."

"But why not tell me?"

"This time the wrongdoer should speak, not the victim," he declared cryptically, and seemed pleased with what he had just said.

"That's not fair."

"*You're* looking for fairness—*you*?!" he retorted, and was gone.

This outlandish accusation, in the heart of Netanya,

made me furious, but I didn't do anything. I was very much alone that year. In fact, I felt consumed by loneliness. On weekends and holidays, the other soldiers would return to their homes while I remained at the base. The heat and the training overwhelmed me. When I got leave for an evening, I would sit in a café and watch the women pass by. I knew not a single man or woman in the town, and any attempt at striking up a conversation was rebuffed. "Piss off!" one woman lashed out at me. "Find yourself a whore, and don't bother us passersby."

The heat and the exhausting training left no room for thought, only for vague fears. I would sit in the café, drink a couple of glasses of lemonade and a cup of coffee, take a walk along the beach, and return to the camp. My loneliness must have been apparent even in the way I walked, because people distanced themselves from me, with the exception of the man who kept accosting me. I was beginning to resent him, and I feared he'd provoke me to violence.

Once I confronted him. "Beat it! If you don't beat it— I'll beat you."

"I'm not afraid," he said, and it was plain that he wasn't.

To my repeated question as to what kind of injustice he was referring to, he refused to respond. Yet I could tell that he had been born in my region, because he spoke the same type of German that we spoke at home.

"When and where did this happen?" Again I tried to get to the bottom of it.

"It's not for us to testify," he insisted, using the plural.

I avoided him and went on my way. Our training was at its most intensive, and even on those nights when they allowed us to leave the camp, I would stay in, because I was exhausted.

One evening, while I was strolling along the beach, my

accuser showed up and again began making his false accusations. I told him to leave me alone but, out of stubbornness or stupidity, he refused to budge. To get him to go away, I stepped right up close to him. He retreated a few paces, and then stood there. I could see how skinny and slight he was, so I held myself back and did not touch him. But when he continued to accost me with his mumblings, my patience vanished, and I grabbed him. He was as light as a sack of straw. I could have picked him up and sent him flying, but for some reason I forced him down, till he lay sprawled on the sand. Though he thrashed about with his arms and legs, he still would not shut up. I could have trampled him with my army boots.

"Shut up!" I was seething.

"My life is worth nothing anyway, so just go ahead and kill me."

"If your life was worthless, you'd shut up." I wanted to provoke him, too.

"Even if that were the case, it'd be no worse than the misery that you've caused."

I don't remember how I replied to him, or how he answered me. The thought that even in his wretched state he was talking logically and still had his wits about him made me so angry that I kicked him. The kick must have been sharp, because it hurt him, yet he didn't cry out. He closed his eyes and bit his lips.

I saw that I would not prevail over him by force. So I said to him, "If you stop annoying me, I'll leave you alone. I have no interest in hurting you."

He didn't reply. He was trying to ease his pain. I let go of him and returned to the base. For a whole month we trained far up in the hills, without any break. We failed in some of the missions we were given and were punished more than once. From day to day the heat intensified, and all thought contracted. Had it not been for the cook, a civilian employee who pampered us with good food, our life in the hills would have been even harder.

One night I remembered that in Italy, in one of the transit huts on our way to Israel, I had seen a wristwatch on the floor. Without thinking, I picked it up and put it into my pocket. When the owner of the watch realized that he had lost it, he cried like a child and pleaded with everyone to return it to him, for it was the only thing left from his home. People around him tried to calm him down and console him. When their words proved ineffective, they said to him, "After living through the Holocaust, how can you cry over a watch?"

But he wouldn't stop wailing. By nightfall, totally fed up, everyone began to snap at him: "You're selfish. You're bad." Upon hearing their words, he covered his face with both hands, like a tired and confused child, and began to drum his legs on the ground. People turned their backs on him when they saw this tantrum; it seemed as if he'd lost his mind.

And I, completely terrified, buried the watch in the sand.

23

FROM 1952 TO 1956, I studied at the Hebrew University of Jerusalem. These were years spent scrambling to fill in the gaps in my education, to find my place within the social and cultural whirlwind that surrounded me, and, most of all, to find my own voice.

My formal education lasted only through the first grade. But in order to get the matriculation certificate that would enable me to attend university, I first had to pass a preliminary examination that included material taught in grade school. Passing this exam would allow me to go on to take the main matriculation exam. This examination was unforgiving: algebra, trigonometry, literature, English, Bible, etc. Material that is usually taught and then reviewed over the course of years I had to cram into a year and a half of study. No wonder I twice failed the mathematics and English components.

This huge effort drained me and left me with no desire to study. I wanted to return to the orchard. That quiet orchard that changed with each season now seemed to me like a well-spring of blessing. I loved the hours I spent alone there, plowing and harrowing the soil, spraying the insects, watching for the fruit to ripen in the spring and for the leaves to fall in the autumn, and then pruning the trees in winter.

But I did not return to agricultural work. This was not a decision arrived at through a rational thought process. Like many Jewish mothers, my mother dearly wanted to see me excel at my studies. She made no attempt to hide her wishes from me, reminding me at every opportunity that I had to study. Just a few days before she was killed, she said to me, "You will be learned." I don't know what she meant by the term "learned," whether she meant that I would be an intellectual or perhaps just an educated man, someone at home with books. At any rate, it was her heartfelt wish that appeared before my eyes when I decided in favor of studying.

But what should I learn? I considered studying agriculture, so as to combine academic studies with a practical application, but there was no getting around it—my inadequate education was an obstacle once again. When I was tested on the principles of chemistry, botany, and zoology, I had so little knowledge that I couldn't even start university studies in the sciences. In my entire life I hadn't ever set foot in a laboratory or looked into a microscope. The man who interviewed me suggested, not without some derision, that I study the humanities.

I signed up for courses in Yiddish. Why Yiddish? My mother tongue had been German, but during the war and after it we all spoke Yiddish. This language still held dim memories of my grandfather's home, my own home, and the war, and it touched something within me as well. Perhaps it represented the response of someone weak, someone who could not face the outside world and so retreated into his shell. Nineteen fifty-two was not a time for love of Yiddish. It had become a symbol of sloppiness, weakness, and the Diaspora. Everyone disparaged it. But it was this attitude that actually drew me to the study of Yiddish. My orphanhood melded into its orphanhood.

As it turned out, intuition did not mislead me. I did not find many students in the Yiddish department. If the truth be told, there were only three of us, grouped around a short man with alert eyes: Dov Sadan. Sadan was precisely the teacher whom I needed at that time—a sharp yet extremely warm person who knew how to take the measure of his students.

In the early 1950s, Martin Buber, Gershom Scholem, Ernst Simon, and Yehezkel Kaufmann were among those who taught at the Hebrew University. All of them had extensive Jewish and secular education, with expertise in all areas of knowledge and in all beliefs. They were fluent in both ancient and modern languages. No wonder we students felt like mere grasshoppers in their presence.

Like other members of my generation who had come to Israel as youngsters, I didn't know how to adjust my experiences in Europe to life in my new country. More precisely, I didn't know how to deny my past. The past lived inside me with a burning intensity, demanding that I give it my attention. Because of this, the university was not simply a place where I acquired specific knowledge; it was also where my consciousness as an individual began to take shape for the first time. It was where I began to figure out where I came from and where I was headed.

The Hebrew University in the 1950s was an odd mixture of teachers who had immigrated to Israel from Germany or who had passed through Germany just before the war, students who had recently been released from protracted army service, and students who were young and not-so-young Holocaust survivors. Though people often considered it a fusty institution, this was not at all my experience. All my teachers had been born in Europe and, like myself, carried within them the pain of two homelands. Leah Goldberg and Ludwig Strauss, to name but two, had much to say about the dichotomy of having two languages and two homelands. They were poets and spoke like poets. From them I learned how to respond to a line of poetry and, indeed, to an individual word, and to understand that every sound has meaning.

I learned both Yiddish literature and Hebrew literature, but I was increasingly drawn to Kabbalah and to Hasidism. Gershom Scholem conducted his lessons like a magician, mesmerizing everyone. Martin Buber was part professor of the German variety and part Hasidic rabbi. Both of them cultivated a circle of admirers. Kabbalistic and Hasidic language spoke to my heart in a much more profound way than did the literature of the Enlightenment and considerable portions of modern Hebrew literature. A sociological perspective was foreign to me. From the very outset, I felt that literature does not provide a suitable basis for sociological analysis. True literature engages what is concealed in fate and hidden in the human soul; it exists in the metaphysical realms.

I constantly struggled to refine my literary voice. Language was now singing within me, but not the right melody. The melody is the soul of all poetry and prose. I knew it, and it pained me. Throughout my university years I wrote poems, but these were more like the howls of an animal who had been abandoned and for years thereafter was trying to find his way home. Mother, Mother, Father, Father: Where are you? Where are you hiding? Why don't you come, why don't you pull me out of this misery? Where is my house, and where is the street and the strip of land that have cast me out? These formed the essence of my cries, and I loaded all the weight and pain upon words like "loneliness," "longings," "wistful-

ness," and "darkness," certain that they were my faithful mes-
sengers and would go straight into the reader's heart.

Prose saved me from this sentimentality. By its very
nature, prose demands the concrete. Abstract emotions and
ideas are not among things that prose likes. Only ideas or
emotions that arise from something concrete can have a
legitimate existence. One has to learn these basic facts very
slowly, and I, with my minimal education, was even slower.
Instead of learning to observe the body and its movements, I
was drawn toward vagueness and dreams.

Like many of my generation at the university, I
devoured the writings of Kafka and Camus. They were the
first prophets from whom I sought to learn. As is the case with
anything one studies when young, my first encounters with
them were superficial. I got enmeshed in the dreams and in
the vagueness, and I didn't see that Kafka's mist was shaped by
detailed descriptions, by precise sensations that strip the mist
of its haze and make the mystery into an "ordinary mystery,"
to borrow Max Kadushin's well-known saying.

Russian literature saved me from these nebulous mists
and symbols. I learned from Russian authors that there's no
need for them: reality, if described correctly, produces symbols
all by itself. In fact, any specific situation can also be viewed
symbolically.

But I'm rushing ahead of myself. For a long time, I was
enthralled by the magic of Kafka. My reading of Kafka was
that he was aligned more closely to Kabbalah and to Hasidism
than to the literature of the Jewish Enlightenment and to
modern literature. But it was only later, when I became familiar with S. Y. Agnon's writing, that I discovered literature
with a real affinity for the mysterious.

My relationship to Yiddish was different, and I sought
to bind myself through it to my grandparents and to their

home in the Carpathians. In the depth of my heart I knew that by binding myself to my grandparents, to the melody of their language, I would be able to bind myself as well to the Jewish sources over which I'd pored with Gershom Scholem and Martin Buber.

I spent my university years searching for an authentic form of Judaism. I didn't content myself with academic studies. I'd spend hours in the religious neighborhoods of Jerusalem, in the small synagogues in Me'ah She'arim and Sha'arei Hessed. I loved listening to toddlers speaking Yiddish, to students chanting in the *heder* schools, and to the prayers in the synagogues on weekdays and on holy days. I was very drawn to this tangible spirituality, but never as someone who wanted to become religious himself. My relationship to Judaism was like that of my teachers—Sadan, Buber, Scholem, and Bergman. Their connection to their Jewish heritage was a post-assimilatory one that was no longer embroiled in the struggle between fathers and sons, but transcended it. Neither Buber nor Scholem was a traditional mystic, but they both had an affinity to Jewish mysticism. Buber had passed his on to Hugo Bergman. Bergman, a philosopher in his own right, translated it into his own language. Without keeping the 613 *mitzvot*, Sadan was an Orthodox Jew.

During these years I became close to Agnon, and we would meet from time to time. I first encountered him in 1946, when I was at Rachel Yana'it's agricultural school. Agnon, who lived in nearby Talpiot, would sometimes drop by. There were fifty of us youths, Holocaust survivors from Poland and Romania. Agnon would sometimes approach one of the children and ask him about the city of his birth and about what he had been through during the war. When I told him that I had been born in Czernowitz, he was delighted. He knew the city well, and immediately began to rattle off the names of people and places there. I had no idea what he was talking about, but his appearance and manner of speech were not unfamiliar to me. He resembled my uncle Mark, whom I vaguely remembered. I was surprised when I was told that Agnon was a writer. There were no telltale signs of this in the way he dressed, no long hair, and no ostentatious necktie. He seemed like a man with time on his hands.

It was only years later that I got to know Agnon's writing, and then I immediately felt close to him. I was thrilled to encounter the names of people, towns, and villages that I vaguely recalled from home. Bukovina and neighboring Galicia had been separated only at the end of World War I, and Father used to talk with great fondness about the Galician towns he had frequented in his youth—Lemberg, Brod, and Buczacz.

Later, when I read Agnon's books—*In Her Youth*, *Tehillah*, and *In the Heart of the Seas*—I knew that he was describing the lives of my parents and grandparents, albeit in a fictional form. I vaguely remembered the peacefulness and the tranquillity that reigned throughout the Hapsburg Empire, in the villages and small cities that we would visit in the summer, and I understood what he was talking about.

In my early attempts at writing prose, I didn't follow Agnon. On the contrary, I strove to cut myself off from the past and tried to insert myself into my new environment. In my first stutterings I was a farmer working in the Judean hills, a kibbutz member, a fighter in the Palmach, a watchman guarding an orchard—anything but what I really was. In those years it seemed to me that I had no identity of my own and that I had to construct or, more accurately, invent one. Through this strange invention I derided those who clung to their memories and were bogged down in the sickness of the past. I was a farm child, not a refugee boy who for years had wandered from country to country, to be finally washed up on the shores of Atlit. S. Yizhar, Moshe Shamir, and Haim Gouri were my role models. Youthful and optimistic literature suited my secret yearning to change, to forget, to transform myself into a "native" Israeli.

Years passed before I came to terms with myself and discovered the work of Agnon. By then I was prepared to accept my own identity. But that coming to terms, like all such processes, was not without pain.

Most of my generation decided otherwise. They invested a huge amount of effort into suppressing and eradicating their past. I have absolutely no complaints against them; I understand them completely. But I, for some reason, didn't know how to assimilate into the Israeli reality. Instead, I retreated into myself.

For this, Agnon served as an excellent role model. It was from him that I learned how you can carry the town of your birth with you anywhere and live a full life in it. Your birthplace is not a matter of fixed geography. And you can extend its borders outward or raise them to the skies. Agnon populated his birthplace with everything the Jewish people had created in the past two hundred years. Like any great writer, he wrote not literal reminiscences of his town, not what it actually was, but what it could have been. And he taught me that a person's past—even a difficult one—is not to be regarded as a defect or a disgrace, but as a legitimate source to be mined.

Unlike many of his generation, Agnon was not engaged in a conflict with previous generations. His youthful rebellion was brief. I don't accept the common claim that Agnon was ambivalent about the Jewish tradition. He was certainly not fond of the religious establishment, of the fossilization, the routine, and the arrogance that can accompany religion, but

the Jewish heritage was extremely dear to him. Year in, year
out, he would study Jewish texts with the diligence of a
scholar. It is true that Agnon reserved a measure of irony and
scorn for pompous people and for any form of vanity or distor-
tion, but in the best of his work he lays aside satire and irony,
and enters the world of his forefathers.

Sadan, Scholem, and Buber were close to Agnon, and
sometimes I would meet them all in a café, on the street, or at
the university. Agnon was the most entertaining. He always
had anecdotes and reminiscences about people from his past
whom he loved to poke fun at, and stories about contemporary movers and shakers and professors who considered themselves intellectual humanists.

What the members of this group had in common was
their post-assimilationist relation to Judaism. Being Jewish
was in their souls. Agnon obsessively collected old Jewish
books, pamphlets, and notebooks. For hours I would trudge
along with him from bookstore to bookstore, sometimes simply in search of a small Hasidic pamphlet that he had heard
had been reprinted. He tried to do the impossible: to connect
Judaism to the modern world.

Zionism for this group was a sort of return to Judaism,
but not an Orthodox one, or one that was in any other way
doctrinaire. Scholem called himself a "religious anarchist."
This description also suited Buber. They sought to raise Kabbalistic and Hasidic texts from their obscurity so as to demonstrate the importance and relevance of these texts to our
contemporary generation. Yehezkel Kaufmann tried to wrest
biblical study from Christian research, and Yitzhak Baer
sought to demonstrate Jewish continuity since the Second
Temple. Dov Sadan presented contemporary Hebrew literature in dialectic terms, as literature that emerges from
the clashes between four ideological streams—Hasidism, the

Mitnagdic opponents of Hasidim, the Enlightenment, and Modernism.

As opposed to the world from which I had come, Agnon's world appeared calm and ordered. I had come from an apocalyptic place, a world that imposed upon my writing a completely different form of language and rhythm. In Agnon's universe, despite the destruction and the great losses caused by World War I, there were still remnants of a cultural edifice and, most important, a Jewish world that had renewed itself in the Land of Israel. But Agnon was nonetheless a guide for me. I felt that in his writing he engaged the entire Jewish experience—its development, its wanderings, and its teachings, both revealed and concealed. If one can say that the writer is the collective memory of his tribe, Agnon embodies this.

The years in Czernowitz and the years of the war formed the synapses of my reflexes and emotions. My university years shaped my critical faculties and sharpened my skill at expression. I was fortunate that the teachers I encountered became my mentors, and even after I finished my studies I continued to see them. They knew of the struggles I went through with my writing, but they never hid the truth from me, and their criticism was not always easy for me to accept. Much later, with the publication of my first novella, *As an Apple of His Eye*, Gershom Scholem grasped the palms of my hands with both of his large hands and said, "Appelfeld, you're a writer."

24

LIKE EVIL SPIRITS, people who know it all seem to be everywhere. When I began to write, it was as if they lay in ambush in every corner. Manuscripts that I would submit to newspapers would be returned to me with venomous comments attached. Editors would invite me in for a conversation just to reproach me in a paternalistic tone for having no talent and would urge me to stop writing. It seemed important to them that I face my limitations and cease to harbor any illusions.

It was not hard to undermine the little self-confidence that I possessed. Some went too far, claiming that I was writing about a subject that shouldn't be touched, that one could record testimony about the Holocaust but not weave fantasies. Later, when my writing improved a little, they claimed, "You're influenced by Kafka and by Agnon. You don't have a style of your own."

Tougher than most of them was my friend D., the son of a professor. A young man with an extremely broad education, he was considered a literary scholar and was fluent in many languages. A full head taller than I, he was, not surprisingly, able to look down on me in more ways than one. I interpreted his way of looking at me as arrogant, and I wasn't mistaken. And yet I still showed him my early writing. I believed that a man with his level of education would be receptive to my work and would either point out defects that I could correct, or indicate the path along which I might develop. He was four years older than I and was considered a genius at the university. His knowledge and his powers of articulation were enthralling; many succumbed to his spell, myself included. In questions relating to the humanities, he had clear, set opinions.

His comments on my short stories were restrained but hurtful, as if I were simply amusing myself by toying with something with which one should not play. This wasn't said outright, but indirectly. His hemming and hawing confirmed what I had long been afraid of: I was aiming at the impossible. Had he said it all in just a few clear sentences, even if they were negative, it might have been easier for me. But he spoke generally, haltingly, as if trying to mitigate any injury he might be causing me. This only clarified what I myself felt: that there was some sort of discrepancy between what I wanted to say and what came out. I noticed that D.'s words were always accompanied by a smile. This smile was harder to take than what he actually said, for it revealed his thoughts: You are wasting your time.

I did have other friends, people who always made the effort to listen to me and help me. They were unassuming types who never put themselves or their egos at the forefront. Always ready with the right word, they would say things that would take root and, later, blossom. When I was in complete despair, their hands would be stretched out, an encouraging word on their lips. They never looked down on me. They knew my weaknesses—which were fairly obvious—but they also saw the great effort that I was putting into my writing. They believed in me and supported me, and they became my writing mentors.

I didn't always know how to learn from these friends; I didn't even always realize that they were my teachers. Sometimes I repudiated them, when it seemed to me that they didn't understand me. Instead, I would display a naïve reverence for the "experts," the language conjurers. They struck me as more important than my modest friends, who had not studied at the university. I felt that, were I to cast in my lot with the scholars, they would open the doors to the Temple of Literature; and that their approval would ensure that my path would be strewn with roses. I eventually learned that they were incapable of friendship; they were much too occupied with themselves, with maintaining their own status and honing their own words, to be able to give something to anyone else.

Now, when I try to remember what D. said to me, I can recall only the flow of his mumblings; everything is abstract, and no one clear picture emerges. The fate of abstractions is that they grab you for a moment and then evaporate. Only words that create pictures can be retained. The rest is chaff. It took me years to understand this, to free myself from the false power of the sneering smile. It took me years to return to the embrace of my loyal, good friends, who knew that a person is no more than a bundle of weaknesses and fears, and that there's no need to add to them. If they know the right word to say, they hold it out to you like a slice of bread during a war. And if they don't, they sit beside you in silence.

25

WHEN MY BOOK *Smoke* was published in 1962, the poet Uri Zvi Greenberg summoned me to him. He must have been expecting someone who looked different. "You're Appelfeld?" he exclaimed.

"I suppose so."

"Never mind, then."

He didn't ask where I was from, who my parents were, where I had been during the war, or what I was doing now. He had some words of praise for my book, though I immediately felt they were rather grudging. He called my work "expression reined in" and sneered at the phrase "restrained writing," which critics had used to describe it. "What is 'restrained'?" he mocked. "If you have something to say, then say it, and say it loud and clear. And if you have nothing to say, then keep quiet."

As for holding things in, he explained to me that other nations could engage in art for art's sake, and they've certainly achieved some notable success in this area. But we Jews haven't been given this skill. At most, we can imitate it.

AHARON APPELFELD

What we have been given are vision and prophecy, and when we tap into them we create something real. A people such as ours cannot permit itself amusing descriptions or nuanced sensibility. We are all links in a generational chain that extends back to the God of Israel and to His Torah, and it is from this we draw our sustenance. Only Jews who have forgotten who they are, who their forefathers were, go astray in foreign pastures. After the Holocaust, this would be the worst thing for us to do. Going astray is a sin. Have we not seen what European culture is, with its ghosts swarming in its cellars? Are we now going to imitate them, write in iambic pentameter, and devote ourselves to descriptions of utter nonentities? At the end of his life, the great Tolstoy understood that European culture was bankrupt, but in his case there was nowhere to go. All that was left to him was a desiccated New Testament; he had to make do with this sparse fare for his remaining days. We Jews, however, have the treasures of the Torah, the two Talmuds, the Midrashim, Maimonides, the *Zohar*. What other people in the world has such a rich heritage? But we have always fled from ourselves and from our role in the world, hiding in the public parks of New York and Paris, as if those places could nourish our depleted souls. Art that doesn't convey the beliefs of our forefathers will not save us. And without this great, all-encompassing belief, the Land of Israel will not save us, either. We must burn all the idols—the Golden Calf and all the other spiritual calves—and return to our forefathers, for without them our existence is worthless. Without them we're little more than imitators, moles, nothings.

I realized that this tirade was not simply criticism of my slight book, but was actually leveled at our entire intellectual enterprise in Israel. From his poetry and from his manifestos, I was familiar with Greenberg's criticism. But it was still difficult not to take it all personally. It was as though I embodied the stubbornness and insensitivity that he had railed against and, instead of aligning myself with my fore-fathers and their beliefs, I was toying with descriptions and nuances in the manner of Chekhov or Maupassant. I was on the wrong path, but because I had only just set out on it, it was best to set me straight now. He spoke by turns gently and loudly, as if trying to pour his thoughts into my obdurate ears.

I have never been particularly fond of either pathos or big words. I loved and I still love to observe. The advantage of contemplation is that it's devoid of words. The quiet of objects and of landscape flows toward you without imposing itself on you. By nature, I'm not demanding of people. I take them as they come. Sometimes I'm moved by weakness no less than by an act of generosity. The vision and the prophecy of which Greenberg spoke have always seemed to me like some ancient mantle of glory in which we can no longer wrap ourselves. But, lo and behold, when he spoke to me that eve-ning Greenberg struck some hidden chords within me. At first it seemed to me that he had exposed my personal disgrace: neither my parents' home, nor the war, the youth movement, the army, or even the university—none of them had been able to connect me with my forefathers and with the sources of their beliefs. No doubt there did exist profound Jewish belief, but I didn't know the path to it.

It's not hard to expose a man's weakness, to instill in him self-criticism and doubt, and that's what Greenberg did to me that evening. He hurt and angered me, but beyond that I felt the tremendous energy that pulsated within him. It was not simply an energy that empowered an individual, but energy of a different sort altogether—a collective flow that seemed to have been channeled into one man and then poured out onto me with these words: "The individual, for all his importance, is not the main thing. The collective must precede him, because the collective is what creates language, culture, and the belief system. If the individual makes his contribution to the collective, he raises the level of the collective and that of himself, too. A creative person who does not have the power to do this will not be included in the nation's memory."

Had he said all this in a well-modulated voice, I would perhaps have taken it better, but because his voice grew louder and louder from one moment to the next, I eventually stopped listening and heard nothing more than gratingly offensive noise.

What a different man Agnon was! Agnon also held fast to his forefathers' beliefs, but his conversations were composed and wise. What Greenberg sought to do by storm, Agnon achieved with silence. I knew Agnon very well. He never voiced direct criticism about my writing; instead, he'd offer double-edged comments that were semi-ironic, sometimes teasing. That evening, Greenberg spoke to me with all the ardor in his heart, as a father speaks to a son. His words were neither measured nor rational, but they were authentic.

That was my only meeting with Greenberg; I never saw him face-to-face again. I would sometimes see him in the street, billowing past like a stormy spirit or standing and talking to someone with great passion. I distanced myself from him. His demands on me were not the demands that I cared to make on myself. But he apparently kept me in sight. On more than one occasion he inquired about me through friends. And more than once he relayed a clear injunction: "Don't get bogged down in small details. Deliver your message loud and clear. One cannot speak of great catastrophes in whispers."

I knew that he truly and sincerely respected me, but I no longer went to visit him, nor did I ever see him again. I was told of his death when I was abroad.

26

A FEW MONTHS before Agnon's death, I passed by his house in Talpiot. A window was open and music blared from it; I felt that something was not right. I hovered near the window but did not dare to knock on the door. Eventually, however, I summoned up the courage and knocked. Agnon opened the door, happy to see me. It turned out that he had been listening to the news and had dozed off on the sofa; the radio had stayed on at full blast.

"How thoughtless of me to have left the radio on!" he said apologetically. "It's good that you woke me up." He went right off to make me a cup of coffee.

Because I so loved his writing, Agnon became my guide through the great confusion I experienced when I began to write. My encounter with the writer himself proved less simple: in Agnon, irony was so deeply ingrained and so sophisticated that sometimes it was hard to detect. Admiring professors and not a few foolish fans flocked to him. No won-der he protected himself with this arsenal of irony. The pity was that this method of expression became so ingrained within him over the years that it became second nature to him, and he could no longer manage without it.

During the 1950s, Agnon was considered the most important writer in Israel. Everyone lavished praise on him. Research was devoted equally to important and trivial aspects of his work. And, as often happens, people almost stopped reading his books. Did he know? Was he aware of this? It's hard to say. He was absorbed in himself, talked mostly about himself, and grumbled about those who stood in his way, who didn't appreciate him as he felt they should, who bombarded him with letters, who were noisy on his street and hampered his writing, or who wrote negative reviews of his work. There is no doubt that he had a generous nature and was extremely perceptive regarding people and their situations. But he never expressed this. What stood out most was his self-absorption.

That evening, Agnon was different, as if he had come out of hiding. He didn't talk on as he usually did, but asked me things and listened to my replies with great attentiveness, as if he had just met me for the first time and was trying to solve a riddle. I told him what I had been through during the war—though not in great detail, for I knew that his attention span was short. But that evening he was apparently eager to hear, because he kept asking for more details. Eventually he said, "What you saw in your childhood would be enough for three writers."

Then he said something unexpected. "When all's said and done, I've spent my entire life among books, either reading or writing. I haven't had it hard—it wasn't as if I had to work my way up from the gutter. Had I been a blacksmith, or a farmer working the land, or a craftsman with a strong connection to his material and his tools, I would have been a different writer."

I felt that he spoke from the heart. For years people have been talking about the symbolism in Agnon's writing, and it turns out that Agnon himself, like any real writer, preferred the tangible to the symbolic.

Several times that evening he questioned me about what I had done to survive alone in the forests, what I had eaten, and with what I had covered myself at night. When I told him about the Ukrainians among whom I had worked, he asked me to say a few words in their language. For his part, he told me many things I had never known about the city of my birth, about its intelligentsia and its rabbis, and about the infamous Jacob Frank, the false messiah, who poisoned many souls by convincing people to sin so as to hasten the redemption.

This was Agnon without his affectations. That same evening, he tried to explain to me what my parents had not been able to tell me and what I wasn't able to learn during the war years. "Every writer needs to have a city of his own," he said, "a river of his own, and streets of his own. You were expelled from your hometown and from the villages of your forefathers, and instead of learning from them, you learned from the forests."

It was almost as if he was trying to prepare me for the days ahead. The irony in his voice receded and a yearning took its place. I loved this voice, for it reminded me of the narrator's voice in his stories.

On that evening, I sat across from an old man, a man in the fullness of his years. He knew that all the honors and compliments that had been showered upon him were like chaff. What would stand the test of time was the voice—a voice without ambiguity or deviousness or irony—that he had inherited from his forefathers, the voice one could hear in his novel *Tehillah*. This was Agnon's true voice. The disguises and the evasions were, in the end, merely outer garments, necessary perhaps to capture the reader's attention, but not the core of what he had to say.

That evening, he spoke to me with the cadences of his forefathers, the sound of which still echoed in my ears from the time I had spent at my grandparents' home in the Carpathians. He spoke to me very plainly and told me that in his youth he had tried to study from one of the Jewish holy texts every morning, so as to draw upon their cadences and their holiness. He couldn't always manage it. Sometimes the books would confuse him. He advised me to study the works of Rabbi Nachman of Bratslav, and not only the stories that were then in fashion, but *Likutei Maharan*, a mystical book full of secrets both divine and human. As he spoke to me, something glowed within him, and I realized that this was an altogether different Agnon, one who still roamed his—and my—native land, the Carpathians, where the Ba'al Shem Tov had walked with his pupils. That evening, he felt that it was important for me to learn where I had come from and where I had to go.

Then he told me about his book *Days of Awe,* over which he had labored for many years so that Jews would find it helpful during the High Holy Days. To his eternal regret, the critics and general public never felt as he did about it.

It was already late, and I rose to leave. Agnon stopped me. "Sit. What's the hurry?" he said. I felt that loneliness was weighing him down and that it was hard for him to be alone. He revealed something else to me that evening—that over the past few months he had been thinking a great deal about his father and his mother. Had he the time, he would have gone back and told their story in a completely different way. He felt there were more than a few defects in his writing that he wanted to correct, but this would have required considerable energy, which he no longer had. In previous years he had been able to stand at his lectern and write for hours, but this was now hard for him. And that's how I parted from him. My heart told me that I would never see him again, and my heart guessed right.

27

DURING THE YOM KIPPUR WAR, I served as a lecturer in the army's Education Corps, and I found myself stationed alongside the Suez Canal. This unexpected war brought back to me, and apparently not only to me, memories of World War II. They surfaced during every discussion. The young soldiers were interested in the most minor details about the war, as if trying to fill in the gaps from those years long past. Unlike their questions on other subjects, the questions they asked about the war were not ideological or arrogant, but were full of empathy and went right to the point.

Children of Holocaust survivors were particularly interested. Their parents either hadn't told them of their experiences or had told them very little. Although they had learned a bit in school, it was always in either a generalized or a frightening way, such as films of Auschwitz.

Long stretches of desert time loomed before us, and we had the opportunity to explore issues that were far from simple, such as the complex relationship between victim and murderer, or the ideas and beliefs that nurtured Jewish intellectuals in the years before the Holocaust. And what were these beliefs? That the world was making progress, moving ahead for the good of all. That if Jews were to leave the narrow confines of their world to put down roots and become part of the larger world, they would be accepted with open arms. That this progress would dispel the poisonous vapors of past hatreds.

Not too many years earlier, Holocaust survivors were confronted—even harassed—by all kinds of bluntly rude questions: Why didn't you resist? Why did you let yourselves be led like lambs to the slaughter? Survivor-witnesses brought in to speak at high schools and youth-movement meetings were set upon with these questions. The survivors would stand in front of these groups trying to defend themselves as the young people attacked them with facts gathered from newspapers and books. On more than one occasion, the survivors would leave feeling guilty as charged.

But it was different now. The passing years had done what passing years tend to do. Ideological convictions had softened or disappeared. Different truths worked their way through the collective consciousness. These soldiers were no longer the youths who had been filled with certainties and arrogance, but young people who realized that life sometimes springs something unexpected on us—such as this present war—and that one should not judge others hastily, to say nothing of misjudging them.

If I'd had some texts to work with, we would certainly have studied them in depth. Such complex issues are hard to grasp without the help of written materials. So I decided instead to tell them about myself. It's not easy to reveal yourself to a large audience. True, a writer always speaks about himself, but the act of writing is like putting on clothing: you don't stand there stark naked. This time, however, I didn't have a choice; without source texts I knew that I would not be able to speak about the usual clichéd approaches to anti-Semitism and the weakness of the Jews.

First I told them about my parents and my city. My parents, modern assimilated Jews, saw themselves as an integral part of the European intelligentsia. They took an interest in literature, in philosophy, in psychology—but not in being Jewish. Father was a successful industrialist and a member of upper-middle-class society. We took pride in the German we spoke and cultivated the language. Even during the late 1930s, my parents deluded themselves into believing that Hitler was a passing phenomenon. There were many signs that indicated the bad times to come—every daily newspaper and every weekly journal revealed the truth—but no one actually believed that things would turn out as they did. Delusion. Holocaust survivors would be accused to their faces of blindness and of self-delusion. But here, on the banks of the Suez Canal, the term "delusion" had a different ring to it. Even our excellent military intelligence had not foreseen this scenario; even our army had misled us.

A different sort of delusion.

For me this was an encounter on two different levels. The stark, bare desert and the soldiers who gathered around me were constant reminders of my wanderings in Europe after the war, and of my first years in Israel. For years I had tried to forge a bond with the desert landscape that I loved from the first moment I saw it. But I didn't dare write about it; actually, I couldn't. My childhood, my parents, and my grandparents had been part of a different landscape. I couldn't uproot myself from the landscape to which they had been connected. When I first arrived in Israel, I was indeed in close contact with the land for four years—looking after trees, which I loved—but the barrier between me and my adoptive landscape still remained. Now, however, amid the sand dunes, hundreds of kilometers away from our homes, all of us felt like strangers who were trying to understand not only what had happened in the Holocaust, but also what was happening here. We had been trying to change. Had we changed? Or had we actually remained the same strange tribe, incomprehensible to itself and incomprehensible to others?

It was not only I who spoke; the soldiers expressed their feelings, too, particularly those whose parents had survived the Holocaust. They resented the fact that their parents had kept their previous lives hidden from them for years, cutting them off from their grandparents and from the language of their grandparents, creating an artificial world around them, as if nothing had happened. I tried to defend myself and their parents. Holocaust survivors had faced excruciating choices, the main one being whether to continue living with the memory of the Holocaust or to start a new life. They had chosen the new life. That choice was not lightly undertaken. They had wanted to spare their children the memory of suffering and the shame; they wanted to raise them to become free men and women, without that dismal legacy.

We should not forget that it was not only the survivors who wanted to repress their experiences; the feeling throughout Israel at the time was that survivors should renounce their past and put aside their memories. During the 1940s and 1950s, religious beliefs and European mannerisms were seen as alien values to be kept out of Israeli life. Both the religious Jew and the assimilated Jew were frowned upon.

In the heart of the Sinai Desert, we spoke of the relationship between Jewish tribalism and Jewish universalism, and whether it was possible to bridge the two. The soldiers, most of them in their twenties, were already equipped with professions and trades and a secular worldview, but they were aware that the roots of our culture are in the world of faith. Without noticing it, we moved from the general to the personal, speaking in groups of two or three. Among the soldiers I found one whose father had been in the camp with me.

The three days that I spent with that unit not only brought me close to the young soldiers, but also gave me a deeper insight into my own life. As in every war, there hovered above us a sense of fate hanging in the balance. Who knew what awaited us?

The voices of the soldiers became more lighthearted and jovial toward the end of my stay. The cease-fire appeared to be holding. I found it hard to part from this unit of young people on whose shoulders rested the fate of a people welcome neither in Europe nor in this part of the world. As different as the struggle was here, it was, nevertheless, the same ancient curse pursuing us.

28

I KNEW MORDECHAI many years ago, when I was in my thirties and a teacher at an evening high school. He had a small grocery store opposite the school. During the afternoon he would close it and prepare sandwiches and coffee, and we would sit by the window and play chess. Chess was his great passion, and it brought out interesting aspects of his personality: logical thinking that was without deviousness. When he lost, a soft glow of embarrassment would spread across his face.

He was my age, but since he was completely bald, worked in a grocery store, and had married early, he already looked forty. Yet the moment he closed the shutters and set out the chessboard on the bench, his appearance would change and a youthful eagerness would sparkle in his eyes.

The game would usually go on for an hour and a half, sometimes two. This shadowy time beside the drawn shutters was intoxicating, making us forget everything, and yet I would notice some movements in him that could not be seen when Mordechai was behind the counter. In particular, there was his way of lowering his head as if he had once known how to pray. Sometimes he would close his eyes, summoning his thoughts. His fingers were long and slender and did not suit his line of work, and for this reason they were frequently injured or bandaged. When the game was at its height, his eyes had a wonderful sharpness. As with many naturally gifted chess players, he was not an open man and spoke little; his expression was alert.

Only after I'd known him for a year did he reveal to me that in his childhood, from age five to age nine, he had lived in a monastery—a very strict one where there were compulsory prayers even at night. His parents had handed him over to the monks and promised that they would soon return to collect him. He waited for them for a few days, and when they did not come, he cried uncontrollably. The monks warned him not to cry, but when their admonishments were ignored, they shut him up in an attic. Mordechai cried until he was completely exhausted. When he finally stopped crying, the monks opened the attic door and served him a cup of warm milk. Since then, he said, he has never cried again.

Mordechai was a man of few words; anything he said appeared to cost him dearly. Had I been more considerate, I would have sat and played chess and asked him nothing. One could see that those years still lurked within his body.

Who were his parents? Up until a few years earlier, he was still waiting for them. He had believed that they were alive in Uzbekistan. This false hope was planted in him by a survivor who swore to Mordechai that he had seen them in one of the communes there. It turned out to be untrue, but he was not embittered. A tranquil air surrounded his movements. He would say only the bare minimum, unhurriedly and to the point.

He told me once that one time, at a moment when great panic had seized him, one of the monks—Father George—told him that there was nothing to fear. Fear was imaginary; it is imagination that creates demons. Only our Father in heaven should be feared. The more one clings to him, the less the fear.

Did it help? I almost asked. I tried to avoid asking. I sensed that a question would hurt him.

Once he told me distractedly, "Life's only a parable."

"A parable for what?"

"For our illusory existence."

"So where isn't life illusory?"

"With God," he said, and smiled.

He, of course, observed neither Christian ritual nor our *mitzvot*, and yet his entire being was suffused with a religious devotion acquired in the monastery. Sometimes it seemed to me that he was waiting for the time when he would be allowed to pray once again. It was the monks who had taught him how to play chess. He played with a quiet, focused concentration that intensified as the game progressed. It was obvious that his years in the monastery endowed him with qualities that I lacked.

At half past three, the alarm clock would bring us back to the reality of Mordechai's store. He would unlock the front door and open the shutters, and the first customers would immediately appear. I would remain seated, watching his movements. Standing behind the cash register, he would keep his remarks to an absolute minimum—numbers and more numbers.

Once he told me that after the morning prayers he would work with the monks in the garden. He loved that work.

"And while you were working you didn't talk?" My tongue wouldn't keep still.

"At the monastery there was no talking."

"And if you wanted to speak?"

"You closed your eyes and said, 'Lord Jesus, save me from sinful thoughts and hide me in the shadow of your wings.'"

Sometimes it seemed to me that his real life was buried in the monastery, and what came afterward was nothing but a form of retreating inside himself. This hiding did not bury his previous life. It in fact preserved it; when he spoke of his childhood, he did not use the past tense. In this way, and not only in this way, we were similar. I, too, have the feeling that one day I will be able to pray. Mordechai's religious sensibility had a solid basis. When he said "prayer" or "fast," he spoke from experience.

He also told me about a stream that flowed alongside the monastery. In the summer, he would go down to it and swim. Everything he related to me or implied had a similar tangible and earthly basis, even when he spoke of spiritual matters.

In 1972, Mordechai left Jerusalem and settled on a farm. I don't know why he left the city. Sometimes I feel that some of his mannerisms have become a part of me, such as when I use words that he used to use. Mordechai never completed high school, nor did he study at the university, but his education at the monastery was absorbed into his soul. His life there put him on the path of self-abnegation, and even now this was his rule: less and less speech. It was as if he felt that original sin is rooted in speech.

29

I RECENTLY RAN into the son of a friend whom I'll call T., with whom I had wandered through Europe toward the end of the war and right after it. We came to Israel together, and we spent some time together in the youth movement. His son so closely resembles him that for a moment I was sure it was T. who was standing before me.

A twenty-seven-year-old electrical engineer, T.'s son had just spent two years in the United States completing his studies. I invited him for a cup of coffee. He's a tall young man, refined and polite. As a youth, he excelled at his studies, and he is now busy doing research. I hadn't seen him since he was in high school, so I was very glad to have run into him.

Fate linked his father to me. The time we were together during our childhood was spent in almost complete silence. We were afraid to speak in our mother tongue, and it felt strange to talk in another language. So for the most part we were silent, or we communicated with gestures. In any event, even though we didn't talk much we were very close friends, and when we talked a bit between one silence and the next, T. told me a lot about his family.

The years of war and the years spent wandering through Europe afterward were years when we children were surrounded by darkness. Life battered us from all sides. We learned to keep our heads down, and if we found shelter we would crawl toward it. We were like animals, though without their daring and aggressiveness. After every beating we would flee. We did not even know how to cry out.

After two years of wandering, we reached the coast of Italy. The sun and the water welcomed us; they were our first friends. On that vast and empty shore the winter within us began to thaw. My friend T. was so excited that he refused to get out of the water, even at night. It was in the warm sea water that we felt the first sensations of freedom, and that the first words burst out of us. And it was there that I saw a Jewish merchant who, with a single gesture of his thin, pale hand, managed to express the essence of the war: What is there to say?

For three months we lived on that beach. We saw and heard a lot, but it was as if our souls were closed. Only with time, and deep in our dreams, did the memories of the things we had seen begin to return in a slightly clearer form. My friend T. and I kept busy fishing. We made nets from rags. And, wonder of wonders, every day we managed to catch a few fish. At night we would light a bonfire and roast them. The night, the water, and the fire flowed through us like a thick, dark stream, and we covered ourselves with it. At the time we didn't know that what we were experiencing was a form of rebirth.

When we arrived in Israel, my friend T. distanced himself from me and seemed to withdraw into himself. When I tried to approach him, he would brush me off. He was struggling with himself and with the demons within him. "Leave me alone," his face seemed to say. "I need to be alone with myself."

Eventually T. left the youth movement and went to work in a shoe store in Tel Aviv. I saw him a few times, but we didn't speak much. It was hard to know if he was happy in his new position, but I did notice some telling signs in his face— a slightly clenched jaw and a kind of pent-up anger.

After our army service the links between us faded even more. Each of us was battling his own demons, and our meetings became more infrequent. T. came from a family of converted Jews. His grandfather had cut himself off from his roots, repudiated his father, and adopted another culture. He went off to study medicine. But during the war no distinction was made between Jews and those who had converted. Converts, too, were imprisoned in the ghetto and sent to the camps. When I met T. during the war he was also eleven years old and, like me, without parents. Like me, he had spent the summers wandering in the forests and sought shelter in winter with any peasant who needed an extra pair of hands. When he told me his name I was astonished; his family had created quite a stir in our town.

My friend did extremely well in business. I was not surprised. Most of us who came to Israel as children after the war met with material success. I am continually astonished by the extent of our accomplishments. There are industrialists, lawmakers, army officers, and scientists among us—most at the top of their professions. Few people would guess that the director of that large factory is a man who was a child survivor, because he is unlikely to speak about it, and in fact tends to hide it. T. is the owner of a shoe factory. They say that his exports have taken off in recent years. He has a house in Herzliyya and an apartment in Jerusalem. I have been a distant observer of his remarkable ascent. During the initial years of his success we hardly saw each other. T. was completely preoccupied by his factory, and nothing else interested him. But in recent years we have begun to talk more about the past—not in a deliberate way, but along with other, more mundane concerns. At one of these meetings T. revealed that he had considered studying at the university and had even registered for a night school that prepares one for the matriculation exams. But it was just at this point that his business started to take off, so he canceled his plans. There is, however, a large library in his home. He is interested in philosophy, literature, the arts, and medicine, and he frequently surprises me with his knowledge. He competes with me, I suppose, and perhaps also with his father and his grandfather, as if to prove that it's possible to be knowledgeable as well as rich.

T.'s son is an engaging young fellow, more like a European Jew than a native-born Israeli. He's got a good head on his shoulders, and he expresses himself with precision.

I told him—I really don't know why—about the forests in which I had spent time with his father. I assumed that his father had mentioned something to him about that period. It turned out that I was mistaken. His father had not told him anything at all. He knew absolutely nothing about the land of our birth, about the place to which we had been exiled, or about what had happened to us there. I was astonished.

"Didn't you ask?" I inquired, rather foolishly.

"I asked, but Father didn't really want to answer."

"Were you told about your grandfather?"

"A little," he said, blushing.

His father had indeed told him very little. This fine young man knew nothing about the mountainous homeland where his father and his father's father had been raised, and where generations before them had flourished. One would have hoped that a remnant of his ancestors dwelt in the soul of this son, but he had no way of knowing it. And there was little chance that his father would now sit down and tell him. Were they to have this conversation now, it would have been strained and out of context. What had not been related at the proper time would not ring true at some other time.

My generation told their children very little about their birthplaces and about what had happened to them during the war. Their life stories had been buried deep inside them before the scars had a chance to heal. They didn't know how to open the gate so as to allow some light into the darkness of their lives; instead, a wall was slowly being put up between them and their children. It is true that in recent years members of my generation have tried to breach this wall of their own making, but their efforts are relatively weak and the barrier is solid; it's doubtful that it can ever be dismantled.

"You never talked with your father about it?" One hears this from time to time.

"We spoke, but always in passing, never in depth." One hears this, too.

I am very familiar with that feeling of superficiality. When you're finally ready to speak about those days, memory grows faint and the words stick in your throat. So you wind up saying nothing of value. Sometimes, by chance, the words start to flow, and then you go on and on as if a blocked channel has been cleared. But you immediately realize that this is a superficial, chronological recounting that does not come from the depths of your being. The words flow, but they reveal nothing. When you've finished, you feel confused and embarrassed.

I told T.'s son about the last autumn that we had spent hiding in the forest, about our efforts to preserve our body heat, and about the bonfire we lit when the cold threatened to freeze us, even though we knew that it might give us away. For a moment it seemed to me that if I could succeed in telling T.'s son the story of the forest as it should be told, he would understand everything that followed. But as if in spite of myself, the words failed me. Everything in my head seemed to evaporate, and I could only repeat what I had already said. "It was cold, and despite the danger we made a bonfire."

"Two children in the forest, it's unbelievable," T.'s son said, as if grasping it for the first time.

And so it was, unbelievable. Whenever you speak about those days, you are gripped by a sense of how *unbelievable* it all is. You relate it, but you don't believe that this thing actually happened to you. This is one of the most shameful feelings that I know. The son of my friend T. was sensitive and attentive, and I really wanted to tell him more. But I just could not begin. The story of my life and the story of T.'s life now seemed like one story—distant, complicated, almost impossible to penetrate. Though I described some things, they sounded banal and, even worse, irrelevant.

"And your father didn't tell you anything?" I kept asking like a fool.

"Almost nothing."

T.'s son knew that his great-grandfather was a renowned physician, a fine man who was devoted to the poor with his heart and soul. But he knew nothing of the bitter, complex struggle that was waged for years between the famous doctor and his father, the famous rabbi. To the doctor came people for examinations or for free medication; to the rabbi came wretched people to be healed from their afflictions. One believed in medications and surgery, the other in prayer and charity. In the forest, between one escape and the next, T. had told me many details about that bitter struggle. Even then I sensed that a similar struggle was being waged within him. To his son he apparently told none of it. This chapter remained T.'s secret, sealed within him.

I sat opposite the son of my friend T., filled with a familiar fear: that the story of our lives—of mine and of T.'s, of our parents' and grandparents'—will soon vanish without a trace. I decided to tell him about the Carpathians, the land of the Ba'al Shem Tov, where our families had lived for generations. He had heard about the Ba'al Shem Tov in high school. Even though he's an engineer, immersed in the practical world, I could tell from his face that I could speak to T.'s son about spiritual things. The words "God," "faith," and "prayer" did not put him off. On the contrary, he seemed to want to know more, but I was having trouble mustering the facts, extracting a single illuminating detail from a mass of generalizations.

I felt my knees shaking, as if I had failed a simple test.

"Your great-great-grandfather was a very famous rabbi," I began. But I immediately felt that I had placed an unnecessary burden on T.'s son, and I regretted it. This young engineer, engaged in research at one of Israel's elite institutes, was already living his own life. His father hadn't known how to communicate his life and the lives of his ancestors to him, yet here was I, in my foolishness, trying to awaken in him some interest, some curiosity. How inappropriate.

Out of politeness, or perhaps to please me, T.'s son asked me something about his great-great-grandfather, the rabbi. I stuttered, feeling cruel and foolish.

30

THERE WAS A CHANGING of the guard at the New Life Club, which was established in 1950 by Holocaust survivors from Galicia and Bukovina. Survivors who for many years had energetically managed the club had grown old and wanted to hand the responsibility over to those survivors who had been children during the war.

The handing-over ceremony was both festive and tense, with speeches given by both sides. Feelings ran high, and of course there were interruptions. The older survivors made the "children" (they were called this even though they were already in their thirties) pledge to look after the place, but, above all, never to forget. The "children" were more restrained. Though they spoke about the need for continuity, they didn't commit themselves. There were a few short speeches, very much to the point, that actually made one shiver because of the painful facts that they recalled.

I remember the club almost from its inception. I was twenty years old and had just completed my army service.

There was no one with whom I was close in Israel, so I'd go
there to drink coffee, play chess, or listen to a lecture. In the
club we spoke Yiddish, Polish, Russian, German, and Romanian. I understood these languages, and the place was a kind
of substitute home for me. Although I never took an active
role, over the years I would often return to it. I knew what
went on there, who was sick, and who had died. The members
of the club also followed what I was doing; they read my stories in the newspapers and read what the reviewers wrote
about me.

During the 1950s, fierce ideological arguments raged
throughout Israel—not only on the kibbutzim but also in private clubs, which sprang up like mushrooms in the cities.
Clichés were bandied about, and grandiloquent slogans were
dredged up from the distant past. People who had been communists in their youth became more fervent in their beliefs.
Revisionists forgave neither the communists nor the left-
wingers. The arguments were not confined to the tables where
people drank tea or played chess. Even outside, in the street,
the members of the New Life Club continued arguing, sometimes far into the night.

Like any other organization, the club had a chairman, a
vice-chairman, a secretary, and a treasurer, as well as chair-
men of various committees. People wanted to wield a bit of
authority and to be given a little respect. And as in any organization, the purpose for which the club had been established
was sometimes forgotten. Members became preoccupied with
assigning various honorary positions, bickered about who
would be what, leveled accusations at one another, and eventually there were dismissals and resignations, as if this were a
regular social club and not a club for Holocaust survivors.

But this was only one aspect of it. The club also ar-
ranged memorial services for small towns and remote villages
that had been wiped out during the war, published memorial

books, held symposiums, and brought in wealthy survivors from the United States and Canada to sponsor the club's activities. There were evenings of Yiddish poetry, and the club even established a literary prize to encourage those who wrote.

During those years at the club, I met some wonderful people—ordinary people who didn't take part in the arguments, didn't seek honors, and demanded nothing for themselves. As they sat at the tables, their eyes radiated a simple love for their fellow man. They spent hours visiting the sick in the hospitals and in various facilities, but they also found time to come to the club, to bring memorial candles for commemorations or refreshments for festive occasions. The catastrophe that they had lived through, rather than crushing their innocence and honesty, had left them unscathed. And more than that, it had actually added a glow to the light that they already carried within them.

So it continued, month after month. And then the German reparations money began to arrive, and again the club was thrown into turmoil. Ben-Gurion was accused by some of having sold his soul to the devil; others argued that the murderers mustn't be allowed to reap profits from the goods and property they had confiscated from their victims. The club seemed about to break apart, but for the intervention of one of the members, who had been head of the Judenrat in his hometown and had come out of the experience without a blot on his character. Although most of the Jews in his town had been murdered, he had managed to save about a quarter of the Jewish population. By virtue of this success, and not this alone, people honored him and listened respectfully to what he had to say. Although the split did not occur, the rancor lingered on. Members formed groups and subgroups, and some people avoided other people, calling them "disgusting" and other rude names.

Those were the years when I would come to the club

almost every evening. Most of the members were some twenty to thirty years older than I was, and yet I still felt at home there. I loved the poetry evenings, conversations, and lectures, but more than anything I loved the faces. The faces reminded me not only of the life I had lost in the Ukrainian steppes, but also of the years before the war. Here I had parents, grandparents, uncles, and cousins. It was as if everyone had gathered together just to be with me.

During that period I wrote some poems, and from time to time I was asked by the board of directors to read them aloud at memorial services. Most of the members of the club liked me and encouraged me. I even won a small grant that covered part of the tuition for my first year at university. But even then, some members were opposed to my writing, claiming that when it comes to the Holocaust one shouldn't play with poetry or weave stories, but should just set down the facts. These arguments had some validity—though perhaps an unnecessary degree of nastiness—and they hurt me, because I already realized that there was a long road ahead of me and I was only at the beginning of it.

Had the proponents of "the facts" been willing to listen to me, I would have reminded them that I was only seven at the outbreak of World War II. The war was etched inside my body, but not in my memory. In my writing I wasn't imagining but drawing out, from the very depths of my being, the feelings and the impressions I had absorbed because of my lack of awareness. I do realize that, even had I known how to articulate these it wouldn't have helped. At that time, people wanted only facts, detailed and accurate facts, as if these facts had the power to reveal all secrets.

I had already learned that people don't change. Even the most devastating wars don't change them. A person becomes settled in his beliefs and his habits, and it's hard for him to shake them off. Moreover, all the moral weakness, the base impulses—the cheating, the undermining, the scheming—not only do they not disappear after catastrophes, but sometimes, I'm embarrassed to say, they seem strengthened by them. In 1953, during the struggle for the position of the club's vice-chairman, this was confirmed. Contending for the position were two wealthy businessmen. They were prepared to stop at nothing, and even resorted to bribes. The members' protests fell on deaf ears: "This is so unpleasant—shame on you! Remember where we've come from; there are standards we should maintain." But passions are always stronger than values or beliefs; it's not easy to accept this simple truth.

AS THE YEARS passed, some members fell ill and were hospitalized, and the board established a schedule for visiting them. Some members passed away, and the board put up plaques in their memory inside the club. Then one of the members, someone who was extremely wealthy, died and left all his property to the club. Immediately a brass plaque was fixed to the entrance, and the club was renamed in his memory. There was a bitter argument over this, too. Some claimed that it would be inappropriate to name a place that had been established in memory of victims of the Holocaust after a rich man who had made his fortune through means that were far from kosher. The board's position was unequivocal: if we scratch deep enough below the surface, we'll find that everyone is flawed.

During the early years of the club, the members would bring their children, particularly on the Sabbath and on Jewish holidays. Many thought there should be a special classroom for the children, so that they could learn about the Jews of Bukovina and Galicia, and about what they had contributed to Judaism and to the world. But for some reason this project was never carried out. The children grew up and stopped coming, and the members eventually realized that it would be pointless to force them. They wouldn't have understood, anyway. And perhaps it was for the best that they didn't know what had happened to their grandparents and uncles and aunts.

There was, however, a boy of around seven—his name was Shmuel—who would join us and listen to the conversations with great curiosity. It was clear that he would continue coming when he grew up. He resembled his father, but, in contrast to his father, who was an alert and active man, the son had a quiet, wondering gaze. It was hard to know if this was a look of curiosity or of simplemindedness. Shmuel, at any rate, did not look like an Israeli child but as if he had been transported from a little town in Galicia.

When my first book, *Smoke*, was published in 1962 to good reviews, most people at the club were very happy and congratulated me. Club members read newspapers with a religious fervor, but not books—particularly not books that touched upon the Holocaust. Those who did read books were not happy with mine. My characters seemed grayish and shadowy to them, obsessed with the past, and living a banal existence. Where were the heroes? Where were the ghetto uprisings? And then there were the more vulgar members who seized this opportunity to remind everyone that I had twice been given a grant for my studies. If this was the result, then surely it was better not to support me . . . But most members did stand by me, encouraged me, and even promised to buy a copy. Only later did I understand: it was hard for some people to be taken back to those places and forced to relive those experiences. The moment I understood this, I was no longer angry.

In 1967, on the eve of the Six-Day War, the club was again thrown into turmoil. Some members who hadn't spoken for years, or had barely spoken, now warned of an impending catastrophe. But most members disagreed. "You can't compare what was then to what's now," they claimed. "Now we have an army, and it's going to smash the enemy."

I was called up for reserve duty, and club members vied with one another excitedly to show their support. People pushed banknotes into my pockets, and one of the less popular members (in part because of his miserliness) actually took off his gold watch, gave it to me, and said, "In my name and in the name of my family." Later I learned that this watch had belonged to his brother, who perished in Auschwitz.

Now I knew that the club was my home. All the criticisms and petty complaints that I had harbored disappeared; it was as if they had never existed. I felt the members' warmth and devotion, and I left for the army full of faith in life.

The period of waiting before the war actually began was long and hard. When I returned to visit the club during one of my leaves, I noticed the ghosts that had again emerged from the shadows—places that had not been mentioned for years were now being brought up again, deportations were again spoken of, together with *Aktions*, and trains and forests.

The optimists tried in vain to calm people's fears, but these were deep-seated fears and they brought to mind images that were hard to obliterate. Even strong people confessed they could not sleep well at night. Some asserted repeatedly that it was all our own fault, brought on by our character flaws. If the whole world is against us, they argued, it must mean that there is something bad inside us. Even having our own state and army hadn't improved us.

When the Six-Day War was over, there was elation; people spoke of miracles and spiritual renewal. One survivor who had become rich in America came to Israel and donated a considerable sum of money for us to build a new wing. The club, which had started out in an old building consisting of two rooms and a simple kitchen, expanded upward and outward. Now there was a library, a reading room, a lecture hall, a lounge, and a cafeteria that served sandwiches, soup, and excellent coffee.

The 1960s were good years for the club. There were study groups on the Bible and "Ethics of the Fathers," and many Yiddish lectures. Books arrived from America and from Canada, and the library rapidly expanded. A professional librarian was brought in from the National Library to teach our librarian new classification methods. Our librarian, who before the war had been a teacher at a Jewish high school in Lemberg, rejoiced over each and every book. The library even boasted a few valuable first editions in leather bindings, which became the pride of both the librarian and our club.

After the Six-Day War, there was the feeling, perhaps because of the physical expansion of the club, that Eastern European Jewish culture had found a good home here, and that the intentions of the Evil One, may his name be erased from history, had been thwarted. The poet S., a well-known figure, wrote an enthusiastic poem entitled "Continuity." He read it aloud in the cafeteria one evening, and everyone identified with it.

But there were also unpleasant incidents, dark spirits in the shape of informers. One of the informers provided the income-tax authorities with a list of members who traded in foreign currency, which set into motion an investigation that rocked the club. This gave rise to all kinds of suspicions and bitter arguments. They finally pointed to one man, K., a modest person with a pleasant manner who owned a little haberdashery. He claimed that he had no connection whatsoever with the tax authorities, that this was purely malicious and vindictive slander, and that the evil instigator would have to answer for his false accusations. But these arguments in his own defense were to no avail; they merely increased the hostility toward him. In the end, a general meeting was called and, by a majority vote, it was decided to suspend K. from the club. At the conclusion of the vote, K. shouted, "You'll have to account for this in the next world. There, not one of you will be acquitted."

While he was still shouting, almost in mid-sentence, the guard grabbed him and threw him outside.

THE 1970S WERE somber years for the club, and not only because of the Yom Kippur War. Some of our most prominent members passed away, and some were put into far-flung old-age homes. The club, which in the past had been filled with people, emptied out. Its activities continued as usual, and a Yiddish study group was even started for the young people. But overall enthusiasm had waned. No longer was there talk about publishing new books, a newspaper, or a quarterly. Much was said about the next generation's not knowing anything about the Holocaust and not wanting to know. Some blamed themselves for not telling their children what they really should have told them. But there was a not insubstantial group that argued against the pessimists with all their might, reproaching them and blaming them for spreading negativity.

Right after the Yom Kippur War, there was great concern that if Yiddish literature was not translated into Hebrew it would eventually be lost forever. And so two members left for America, Canada, and Argentina, in order to raise the money to hire a team of translators to translate works of literature from the *mamaloshen* into the language of eternity. The fund-raising campaign was only partially successful.

In 1974, the actor R. arrived from America together

with his sister and his two nephews, also actors. They were immediately made to feel at home in the club. R., a cut above the rest, loved his fellow Jews and their mother tongue. In his youth he could have been an actor in the Polish theater or, later, in the American theater. Theaters all over the world courted him, but he stayed loyal to his native language and to his sister and his two nephews. Together they traveled from place to place, giving performances. Since the end of the war, he had become quite fanatic in his devotion: he would perform only in Yiddish plays.

As soon as R. and his family arrived, they staged *The Dybbuk* and other classics of the Yiddish theater. Besides being an excellent actor, R. was also a remarkable speaker. America, he maintained, was a land of false values. Only in Israel could Jewish culture be born anew. To everyone's delight, not only did Holocaust survivors come to his performance, but young people as well. The club celebrated late into the night. The cafeteria was full to bursting.

During the 1970s, I struggled hard against the emergence of childhood memories that I had buried for years, while also struggling with the form of the novel. These were the years during which I wrote, among other books, *The Age of Wonders* and *The Searing Light*. I would read passages from these books to the club's librarian, who was well versed in modern literature and sensitive to words and their nuances. He taught me an important lesson in the difference between the essential and the peripheral. The university is an important institution of learning, but it's not a school for writers. Literary development takes place through internal conversations, or in conversations between you and those who are your spiritual soul mates. The librarian knew me better than I knew myself.

He knew what bothered me in a text even before I

could point the spot out to him. He always found the hidden flaw. It was strange: we never spoke about content. His belief, like mine, was that the choice of words, the composition of sentences—the narrative flow—are the heart and soul of a work; the rest comes by itself.

During the early 1980s, there was still more thinning out at the club. Power struggles, however, did not let up, even though it was obvious that the veterans would not be able to hold on for much longer. The time had come for those who had been children during the Holocaust to fill the leadership positions. And yet the old board still managed to publish two thick memorial albums, and R.'s theater troupe staged two new performances. But looming over everything were the voluble complaints of the cafeteria manager, who said that the daily proceeds were negligible and threatened to leave if he was not given a subsidy. The veterans reminded him that in prior years the cafeteria had been so profitable that he had been able to build himself a fancy home. But the cafeteria manager replied that he had built his house with his own hands, brick by brick. Had he been dependent on the money he had earned from the cafeteria, he would have still been living in a hovel.

By the end of the 1980s, very few original members were left, and there was great concern about the library and the artifacts in it. Some members suggested turning the place into a synagogue where daily classes would also be held, but the atheists who had been members of the Bund and the rest of the left-wingers were totally opposed to this idea and threatened to enlist the help of their friends abroad. It was a stormy argument. Eventually the matter was dropped.

Around that time the board decided to resign, and a new administration was elected. On the new board were survivors who had been children during the Holocaust and who didn't remember a lot about it. They didn't even remember their parents. When they arrived in Israel they had avoided the club and even scorned it, but when they grew up they understood that, even though they had been children during the war and did not recall very much, they still belonged to the club.

The ceremony marking the handing over was emotional. Obviously close to tears, two members of the departing board talked about the place that this home had filled in their lives and in the lives of all its members, about the activities that had been held there during the past forty years, and about what they had planned to do but could not accomplish. The executives of the new board were more restrained and did not speak for long. One of them, however, revealed that he was only three when the war broke out. His parents had handed him over to a convent, and there he had grown up. There were no other children at the convent, and for years he was afraid that he would remain a dwarf. The nun's reassurances that he would eventually grow up and look like everyone else there did not allay his fears. "I cannot remember my parents," he added, "or my home. Had not the Mother Superior written down the names of my parents, I wouldn't even have known that."

He concluded with a strange comment: "Orthodox Jews discovered me after the war, took me from the convent, and brought me to Israel. I don't want to speak ill of anyone, but I'll just say that my life with them was not a happy one."

There was a deafening silence in the hall; we all sensed that removing him from the convent had shattered his life and that he had never healed.

The new board did not have an easy time of it. The veterans were constantly trying to undermine it, raising counter-proposals at every general meeting, pointing out its mistakes, claiming that its executives were not true Holocaust survivors, that they had been children, and that because children did not remember, it was as if they hadn't been there. The new board was ready to tender its resignation, but there was no one to resign to.

Activities at the club continued to dwindle. The actor R. and his troupe fell afoul of the Israeli cultural authorities and returned to America—but not before they had caused a scandal. They publicly called Israel "a land that devours its inhabitants, full of vulgarity and devoid of culture."

To its credit, the new board did try to breathe new life into the club. Schoolchildren were brought in, and the veterans told them about their experiences during the war. Even a few tourist groups from abroad were brought to the club. The cafeteria manager once again threatened to close the place down if he didn't receive a subsidy. The board placated him with a generous sum.

But despite all the renewed efforts and the contributions that kept coming in, the debts continued to pile up: expenses were greater than income. At the end of the 1980s, the general membership decided, though not by a large majority, to sell the building to the Sha'arei Hessed Yeshiva, and with the money received to pay off all the accumulated debts. If any money remained, it would go toward publishing more memorial volumes.

Thus the life of the New Life Club came to an end. There were those who congratulated the board on the deal, and there were those who, without mincing their words, berated it. The board had seen to it (it was also stipulated in the contract) that the library and the room containing the Judaica collection would be closed until we decided what to do with them. The memorial plaques put up in memory of the donors would not be removed by the new occupants, and there would always be a memorial candle lit in the entranceway. The agreement did not take effect immediately—there were sticking points on both sides—but eventually the contract was signed.

Ever since the club closed, I have avoided the street where it used to be. I think that part of me still lives there. One of the club's veterans, a man with whom I loved to play chess and whose stories about his life during the war I loved to hear, said this: "Better a yeshiva than a billiard club. In a yeshiva at least they pray and pore over the old books." I didn't know if this was a complaint or a coming to terms.

With the closing of the club, I lost a home. But I still keep up with some of the members. Some write me long letters—part monologue and part criticism of my new books, and naturally filled with advice—but this can't compare to the evenings we used to spend over a chessboard or at a game of poker. During a game many things would become apparent about the players: who is trustworthy and who cheats, who behaves nobly and who is a lowly hypocrite.

I spent many hours over the chessboard with Hirsh Lang, one of our most delightful members. An expert player, he would bring great passion to each game. Hirsh had the naïveté of a child, but he was a magician at the chessboard. His games sparkled with clever ploys, innovations, and surprises. He would sometimes play simultaneously against seven or eight people—and win, of course. When he won, a shy, almost childlike smile would spread across his face. His personality and his character emerged only during his game. He was not at all well spoken, and whenever he was addressed he would blush, stutter, and with great difficulty put a few words together.

After the club closed, whenever I ran into Hirsh on the street I would invite him over for a cup of coffee. He invariably carried a pocket chess set with him, and he would immediately suggest that we play. He was never arrogant and never played the part of the grandmaster. During a game he would cradle his head in his hands, lost in thought, as if you were his most challenging opponent. But you knew in your heart that he was doing this only for your benefit, to show a little respect for your efforts. For his part, he had no need to make any effort at all.

People did not treat Hirsh with respect. He earned his living as an accountant, preparing annual reports for the income-tax authorities. He did his work with professionalism, honesty, and discretion, but all these excellent qualities did not bring him much money. People cheated him or didn't pay him on time, and he, out of pure goodheartedness, did not chase them. He lived in a cramped room next to the old central bus station.

In recent years, although Hirsh's economic situation improved, his loneliness deepened. He began to look shabby and stooped. Once I asked him if he had ever gone back to visit the club.

"No," he said bashfully.

"Why not?" I asked.

"What would I do there?" he replied.

Hirsh had come from a very assimilated family, and whenever he was asked about something pertaining to Judaism, he would blush, flinch, and stammer that this was foreign territory to him. He would occasionally summon the courage to ask me about a custom or a commandment, but it would sound as if he were asking about something that was forbidden.

SOMETIMES IT SEEMS to me that all my writing derives not from my home and not from the war, but from the years of coffee and cigarettes at the club. The joy I experienced when it was in its heyday and the pain that I felt when it collapsed—these feelings are still very much alive within me.

Every member carried within him a double and sometimes a triple life. I borrowed a little from each of their lives. In the club there were all types of people: fat and thin, tall and short. Hirsh Lang stood head and shoulders above everyone else, but his height gave him no advantage. He would walk stooped over, as if he was trying to be no taller than the other members. By contrast, our vice-chairman, who was also tall, invariably used his height to dominate everyone and to prevail on every issue.

Those members who were close to me read my work and offered intelligent comments. There were also members who were expert poker players, among them businessmen who routinely conducted secret deals worth many thousands of dollars. These men were skilled entrepreneurs who had raised their profession to a fine art, amassing fortunes along the way. And there were the arrogant, insincere, and empty types who had not been affected at all by the war and its horrors, who would say, almost in spite, "We won't change. That's how we lived before and that's how we'll always be."

Among the rest were the silent ones, those who barely uttered a word. The steam from the coffee and the haze of the cigarette smoke enveloped us for years and brought us to where we are today.